MW01673851

Empath & Psychic Abilities Development: The Highly Sensitive Person's Blueprint, Develop Intuition & Telepathy, Tarot Cards & Readings For Beginners + Healing Guided Meditations

By Spiritual Awakening Academy

About the Author

Emmy, also known as 'Medusa Writes' (@MedusaWritesGla) is a Biological Scientist, turned Teacher turned Writer. Emmy has always experienced the paranormal and been deeply drawn to the occult, knowing there has to be more than this. Emmy studies Astrology and Tarot in their spare time, applying those skills daily.

Emmy states "I have always been a sensitive soul. I came to the conclusion at the age of 27, that I had a different neurotype, most likely autistic/ADHD. I always had a running internal monologue and often recall telling myself to "shut up" as a child, especially

when I was suffering from one of my many, many headaches and migraines. I have also heard voices internally that do not belong to me. Like others, I jumped on the panic wagon and thought I was losing my mind. As I began to heal, repressed memories surfaced. I remembered I had heard things before as a child. I had a gift and had a frightening experience that terrified me so much; I closed myself down to all intuition.

We need to address our psychic state in order to provide adequate support for young people, as the current state of affairs requires more sensitive and empathetic people to turn the tide. As I started to heal, I realised that spirituality is truly the roots and trunk of the tree, and the branches are religions in their many varieties. Some can connect directly to the source through being spiritual. It is my personal opinion that religion can be restrictive, especially when we look at the treatment of women and LGBTQIA+ folk because the message from the source has been rewritten and diluted, often by the male gaze".

Julia Evelina Smith Parker, a classicist, was the first solo AFAB to translate the bible after recognising the failed prediction from Rev Miller was based on biblical passages. The male gaze skews many classical and religious texts. Demetra George wrote "Mysteries of the Dark Moon: The Healing Power of the Dark Goddess" and references evidence of matriarchal society and female worship long before Abrahamic religions such as Islam and Judaism. I am not here to attack the divine masculine; we need you to embrace the feminine in order to improve society. Intuition and creativity are synonymous with sexual intimacy. Shame is a cloak we were given to wear. Embracing your truth and gifts requires a multifaceted approach. Please read on if this interests you.

Table of Contents

Introduction - The Empath Blueprint

A blueprint is a technical drawing: the original from which the additions can be built upon using tracing paper. In the context of this book, I am referring to the blueprint of empaths and Highly Sensitive People found in every century; Jesus Christ – a historical giver and teacher, Harriet Tubman – slavery abolitionist and underground railroad freedom fighter, rescued and freed over 70 enslaved people in the United States. Florence Nightingale came from a rich family and went off to work as a combat nurse during the Crimean War. She became the founding mother of modern nursing through her approaches and techniques. She too was a known empath and would often do the night rounds earning her the name, "the lady with the lamp."

Modern day empaths and highly sensitive individuals are instantly recognisable: Nelson Mandela, Malala Yousafzai, Greta Thunberg – these people care. They care about other human beings, animals and the environment. They too have experienced hardships in their lives, like the empaths of the past.

Let us dive into the blueprint that makes up empathetic individuals and highly sensitive people, starting with the former President of South Africa, Nelson Mandela. Many do not correlate empathetic people and assertiveness, but the two can absolutely co-exist and, this is how a revolution is born.

Famous Empaths

Nelson Mandela

Nelson Mandela's favourite quote from the poem "Invictus":
"I am the master of my fate, I am the captain of my soul" - William Ernest Henley.

Nelson Mandela spent 27 years in prison for his work towards dismantling institutional racism and leading anti-apartheid strategies. A university graduate with a law degree, he was voted into a public service role and proceeded to instigate change from his position of power. In South Africa, this caused mass outrage. He spent 18 years in a brutal prison, located on a small island. Nelson Mandela was able to get hold of a book by Roman Emperor, Marcus Aurelius and adopted the attitude of a stoic.

An incredibly decorated man, he received the Nobel Peace Prize and continued to work for the people after his release from prison. In 1994, he became democratically elected as the President of South Africa and brought about reconciliation from the apartheid.

"During my lifetime I have dedicated myself to this struggle of the African people. I have fought against white domination, and I have fought against black domination. I have cherished the ideal of a democratic and free society in which all persons live together in harmony and with equal opportunities. It is an ideal which I hope to live for and to achieve. But if needs be, it is an ideal for which I am prepared to die." - Nelson Mandela in 1964.

Malala Yousafzai

"I tell my story not because it is unique, but because it is the story of many girls" – Malala [DATE]

Born in Pakistan in 1997, Malala was born a female which is not always a cause for celebration in her culture. Fortunately, Malala's father was a school teacher for girls and gave her every opportunity that was offered to her male counterparts.

In 2008, she could no longer attend school due to the Taliban taking over her town. Extreme law known as "Sharia" which is not commonly practised in Islam was brought into power, and this excluded women and young girls from education. Many citizens of the town were not permitted to have a TV.

Malala spoke out against the injustices her town was experiencing and the misogyny which interferes with girls' education. In 2012, there was an assassination attempt on Malala's life. Fortunately, she survived and awoke with a gunshot wound to the head in a hospital in Birmingham, England.

In 2014, making a new home with her family in England and recovering from physio and surgery, Malala decided: “It was then I knew I had a choice: I could live a quiet life or I could make the most of this new life I had been given. I was determined to continue my fight until every girl could go to school”.

Malala received the 2014 Nobel Peace Prize for her work in securing girl's education rights. Malala has since graduated from Oxford University with a degree in Philosophy, Politics and Economics, and continues to make education accessible for young girls.

Malala is an example of a highly sensitive individual, she has a particular affinity for lifting up other women and constantly moves towards her betterment of self, thus influencing the collective.

Greta Thunberg

In this paragraph, I will refer to Greta as an autistic person, as this is how we identify. We don't have autism: our entire being is forged on top of the neurodivergence; autism *is* us! Greta is most likely both an empath and a highly sensitive person, due to the nature of autism. Autism has mistakenly been thrown in with other personality disorders where a person does not feel empathy, autism is quite the opposite. We can feel so much, it hurts, which is exactly what Greta experienced from a young age.

Often in the autistic community, many of us have special interests or a passion that becomes a lifetime's work – Greta's is environmentalism. At the age of 8, she turned vegan and refused to fly on aeroplanes due to the huge carbon footprint of the meat industry and aviation industry. Greta suffered from an eating disorder due to her extreme suffering over the state of the Earth and our climate emergency. Greta has since learned to transmute this energy into her activism.

The now 18-year-old started protesting at the Stockholm parliament in 2018, three weeks prior to the state elections and started to gain support as each day passed. Greta missed school and her message became "SCHOOL STRIKE FOR CLIMATE" and "Fridays for Future", inspiring millions of others to join her in holding large corporations responsible for their actions towards the environment.

Named as "TIME MAGAZINE person of the year 2019", Greta then spoke at the United Nations:

“You have stolen my dreams and my childhood with your empty words…We are in the beginning of a mass extinction, and all you can talk about is money and fairy tales of eternal economic growth. How dare you!”

Tears fell from Greta’s eyes as she spoke. You can hear the compassion and empathy in her voice, you can hear the urgency, and she is correct – we are leading our younger generations into a baptism of fire. There will be heat emergencies like we saw in the 2020 Australian wildfires, food shortages, mass segregation as we point the finger at each other instead of the giant conglomerates such as Shell and BP.

Climate change and Indigenous people

Much of the land that white people live on, Kanata (which is the first nations name for Canada) for example, has been colonised. Canada was colonised by the English and French which interrupted the way the natives took care of the land. Indigenous people such as the Inuit tribes in Northern Canada and Alaska hunt seals and whales, and have always done so. The difference however between their practices and that of corporations, is they use every part of the animal. Nothing goes to waste, and they are respectful to the Earth. Veganism is a brilliant option if you can afford it, but we cannot force veganism on indigenous cultures when so much has already been taken from them. Freedom of choice to practice life as you please must be granted to all. The meat industry could learn so much from tribes and pay them for their time and knowledge, making reparations and also combating climate change.

We are also now witnessing the emergence of Indigenous people who are reaching far ends of the globe through social media. I learned about some of the First Nations practices through TikTok star @NotoriousCree who dances for his people at Indigenous events.

Indigenous folks have the original ways of looking after our earth. They hunted, grew crops, managed their medicines as well as promoting spirituality amongst the tribes. In Native American culture, two-spirit is an indigenous expression which describes a person's gender identity where they embody both masculine and feminine energies. This term can be found in the LGBTQIA+ community where many labels overlap. Indigenous people have the autonomy to choose how they wish to present with cultural labels outside of colonialism, and also within. However, this expression was not always safe and homophobia and transphobia is still rampant across the globe, as is cultural appropriation. For example, this would be a white person using the term but having no ancestry or lived experience within the indigenous community, and using it because they think it's cool or trendy.

In every indigenous tribe around the world, each has set ways to manage the environment and their tribes. So we have to ask, what has colonisation done to the Earth?

Here are the answers, and many of these are still happening in 2021:

- Mass murder, genocide, rape and kidnapping of indigenous folks
- Colonising native land for agriculture, destruction of sacred lands and homes
- Native people are not allowed to manage their own land
- Residential schools were only recently outlawed, still in operation into the 1990s, and the abuse, including sexual abuse, was rife. There were recently 217 bodies found at a residential school which is now at a body count of over 1000 children, at the hands of white people (particularly Christian nuns).
- Cultural appropriation of Two-spirit, cultural clothing and sacred headdresses used to adorn Chiefs / other decorated members

I believe, in order to restore the world to its natural balance, we have to consult the Indigenous people and ask for their help and forgiveness. Invite them to the table with the scientists and people of power, and place Indigenous folks in those positions too. This is how we begin to achieve equity and equality.

Jacinda Arden's cabinet in New Zealand employed the first female Maori foreign secretary with the traditional Maori face tattooing, which is a start in terms of representation for Indigenous women in politics. We must acknowledge that white colonialists put indigenous people in a place of oppression and disparity and this means we must lift up women of colour and listen to their needs. We do not need to fix things for them, but be supportive when called upon and actively work to be anti-racist and anti-misogyny.

Nanaia Mahuta fights for iwis (iwi meaning nations) with the Treaty of Waitangi settlement, challenging the government to account for its historic wrongs against Ngāti Maniapoto as well as her government duties. For things to change, countries must have a compassionate and empathetic leader, who makes choices based on morals, values and ethics instead of how fat their bank account will get. We as people must remember that the government works for us, not the other way around.

The western notion of a work ethic is one where we grind ourselves into illness and stress, working long hours at unfulfilling jobs within a capitalist wheel.

New Zealand and Iceland recently cut their working week to 4 days and saw a vast improvement in many facets of society.

If we change our environment, working weeks and how we socialise for the better, the empaths and highly sensitive people of the world will feel a dramatic shift in their well-being. It takes a village to raise a child, so why are we expecting a single parent to do that and still work a full-time job? Why are we working 40 hour weeks to have 2 days at the weekend, where you feel absolutely exhausted and don't want to do anything or see anyone? The work mentality is where you must socialise with colleagues and bosses, throwback drink after drink to be with the in-crowd and avoid a difficult work-life with toxic people.

Are we friends with people at work or school? Or do we see them 5 days a week and tolerate them, mistaking it for a friendship when it is an acquaintanceship?

Following on from capitalism, something we are all currently trapped in, empaths and highly sensitive people also struggle with interactions at work. The questionnaire also asks about areas of your personal life. It is a brief approach to finding out if you are empathetic, highly sensitive or both, but mainly you will resonate deeply with chapters of this book. That is the confirmation you need.

Empathy Questionnaire

Can you relate to the following statements?

1. You are tired after making small talk at work and find socialising with colleagues draining
2. You prefer to wear headphones on the morning/afternoon commute
3. The thought of someone sitting next to you and starting a menial conversation fills you with dread
4. You require uninterrupted alone time after socialising
5. You feel burnt out if you do not get this uninterrupted alone time
6. You can read a room within seconds by "feeling the atmosphere"
7. You can tell when a person's energy shifts and wonder if you've upset them
8. Bright lights, loud sounds and extreme textures can be disruptive to you
9. Strangers open up to you, or you quickly get someone's life story/traumas

10. Airports and flying are incredibly draining experiences for you

If you answered mostly yes to these statements, you are very likely an empath or highly sensitive person.

How To Cope as an Empath

Feeling everything becomes draining. At some point you may be overwhelmed with the daily practices of life, and all the people that surround you. Fatigue and reports of feeling drained are some of the most common symptoms shared amongst empaths and sensitive people.

First, it takes some work to remove things that aren't serving you. Many of us are attached to phones, people, food and it's vital to identify what is good for you, personally, and what is not.

By implementing these techniques quickly, you should see a vast improvement in terms of energy. Social media is an energy expenditure; talking to people expends energy. If you can manipulate it then life becomes much more manageable, but more on this later in the book.

Elimination diets

When I say elimination diets, I am not talking about food here. I am referring to behavioural practices that may be affecting you detrimentally as an empath. This will be further discussed later in the book, with techniques to implement better practices to maintain your well-being.

Eliminating, or at least a reduction, in the below actions can immensely help your well-being:

- Reduction of electromagnetic frequencies – phones, laptops, electric devices that we interact with on a daily basis.

- Reduction of socialising and increased journaling about how you are feeling around particular individuals, are there any boundaries that need to be implemented? Or must a person be eliminated from our lives for us to thrive? (By eliminated I do not mean swimming with the fishes!)

- A reduction in commuting to work has seen mental health issues DECREASE, as people have been working at home over the course of a pandemic. They no longer want to travel an hour each way in a sardine can and I do not blame them.

By removing or reducing certain stressors, we can better manage the other areas of our lives.

Finding support safely

With the dangers of social media ever present, it is vital to protect yourself spiritually online as well. Never ever post a picture of your altar online, as some may use it to send you their bad vibes. I generally don't vibe with this but at the same time I protect myself using this knowledge and pass it on to you, dear listener.

Online, not everyone is who they say they are. Please never give out any delicate information and use your common sense alongside your intuition to ensure that the people you are communicating with have your best intentions at heart. There are many wonderful online communities with great moderators to maintain the status quo.

Spiritual churches and yoga studios are good ways to meet like minded people. Again, if something seems off it most likely is. If you visit these places, trust your body to alert you to anything "off." Like many religious institutions, spiritual churches are not excluded from toxic individuals, out to take what they can get. It is essential for you to protect yourself and identify these behaviours to protect others. Many churches have been exploitative in the past, and I'm not only referring to christianity, it has insidious roots in many theologies and religions.

In the meantime, there are wonderful teachers online who can help you access spirituality, if you protect yourself, do your research, and trust your instincts. For example, Shaman Durek is a sixth generation shaman and is an online coach. He also runs an Instagram account and often takes part in "Instagram Lives" where he explains topics in depth and invites other spiritualists on to the calls, which may be a starting point for you if you are looking for online communities.

In the chapters to come, we explore empaths in relationships and how they can often fall victim to energy vampires and narcissists as this is a typical issue for sensitive people and empaths.

Empathetic people and Highly Sensitive Individuals are often the butt of jokes or severely misunderstood. Many of our peers do not realise what we experience on a daily basis. The key to harnessing your power is protecting yourself, which will be discussed in detail and supported by guided meditations at the end of this audiobook.

As always, only take what resonates and leave the rest for someone else. There may be some hidden gems in here for you or something that you might pass on to a loved one. Regardless, thank you for being here.

Chapter 1 - Psychology and Empathy

First, we must identify the differences between introverted individuals, empaths and highly sensitive people (HSP). These terms have been used interchangeably, but there are differences. There are some great resources online that offer quizzes to help guide you. MBTI psychology tests will also measure the levels of introversion and extraversion. Dr Carl Jung was a genius, both scientific and spiritual and his work on integrating the shadow and the anima/animus of our psyche is phenomenal. Here are the definitions of terms used in this book.

Introversion: A personality type where people energise themselves through alone time, where the individual ponders and problem solves internally. A common myth is that introverted people are shy; this is not the case. Introverts are fabulous observers and try to make intelligent decisions, which sometimes means staying quiet and saying nothing!

Empath: A person who is aware and deeply affected by the emotions of others, particularly loved ones and close friends. This could be an innate quality or learned, as many trauma survivors grew up in an emotionally unstable home. Having the ability to predict a "caregiver's" mood is a life-saving skill for many. Some are naturally gifted empaths and have better control, not allowing others emotions to overwhelm them. However, a wounded and untrained Empath will likely experience chronic pain, chronic fatigue, migraines, physical illness and mental health at some point during their life, as there hasn't been a powerful emotional release. Emotional pain and unhealed traumas tend to manifest as disease. Empaths can be introverted or extroverted, depending on their personality and life experiences. Empaths can also identify as a "Highly Sensitive Person" or HSP.

Highly Sensitive Person: Someone who is aware of the details that others may find irrelevant or mundane. HSP's can identify patterns and symbols and form them into thoughts. The Universe sends signals all the time and a HSP is conscious of this. They can hear the fridge buzzing or the TV on standby, feel the tension in the air at an awkward family reunion, have trouble with digestion and processed foods; HSPs are overstimulated by many things. They also tend to be introverted to manage the overwhelm experienced daily but can be deeply empathetic people.

Traits and symptoms found in Empaths and Highly Sensitive Persons' tend to cross over. As an Empath, you will feel the disturbances and changes in the emotions/ feelings in those around you. An

HSP will be affected by their physical environment, and if you are both - then this ebook should find you well.

So what does this mean exactly?

Empathy is a gift and being highly sensitive is a power, in my opinion.

It is the primal creature within who gets goosebumps, sensing unseen danger—identifying when the most minor things are out of balance, such as the drop in barometric pressure. So many of us are affected by incoming storms that we suffer from pain and migraines. Coupling this with the ability to pick up on the emotional environment, it is very, very overwhelming and over-stimulating. Fortunately, as more of us begin to wake up to our gifts and the universe, we find ways to soothe ourselves using nature's gifts, community and introspection.

Have you ever been in a room and the lights flicker? Do these phenomena follow you? Everything is a message, and the sensitivities allow us first to acknowledge this and integrate the learning. The science stands, magnetism and physics are solid theories with evidence, and yet, there are some things we will never understand but have to accept. Energy is neither created nor destroyed, which begs the question, where does it go? Below are tips to help manage whilst integrating the learning in this book.

Everything is energy; what do you expend yours on?

Think of a time where the mind, body and soul felt drained. What nurtured them back to health?

Your energy moved elsewhere and the self-care brought it home. Self-care has a range of practices, whether it be movement and exercise or a hot bubble bath alone. We must replenish our energy to maintain long and happy lives.

Physics teaches us that everything is energy. Atoms, neutrons, electrons and protons are the basis for life on Earth. They do not know entropy as humans do; atoms can have a half-life that is half a billion times the current age of our Universe.

Energy is the currency, not money. Therefore, it is sacred and must be used wisely. I've learned over a series of lessons about what drains me personally, and it is social interaction with people who don't vibe with me. This may resonate with you too. Other people may need 12 hours of sleep to function fully and struggle when this is disrupted by external forces. Balance must be found and so, this individual may have to set time away for a nap during the day to manage their energy levels. Only you know what is needed - feed your soul.

Protect yourself always - reduce screen time and set boundaries

Empaths and HSP must protect themselves spiritually, emotionally and physically to harness their gifts without being overwhelmed or hurt. Experiencing a constant state of stress which isn't even yours to carry is too heavy. This ebook will offer different options of protection; please take what resonates and leave the rest.

First and foremost, try and leave your phone for periods during the day. We have a dopamine response in our brain every time we get positive input, which quickly comes in the form of social media. This creates an addictive response, and we check our phones more often, to the point of endless scrolling.

Secondly, energy can be spent here as people are accessing you through social media, whether you are messaging friends or potential love interests. No one is worth your rest. Text them back tomorrow when you feel rejuvenated.

Many people are affected by the blue light in our technology and the electrical side of things. Charge your phone away from the bed or turn it off during the night.

Master your vulnerabilities and learn to harness this as a gift

This ebook will help you develop skills to manage the problematic aspects of being an empath or HSP. Taking care of yourself and trusting your intuition opens the soul to more experiences, and as a result, some develop psychic gifts. This ebook offers information on the esoteric and honing skills in the areas of Astrology and Tarot and trusting the self through practising techniques used in therapy. Identifying, feeling and releasing emotions help maintain a healthy physical body too, this is often overlooked.

Empaths and HSP - sensitive to psychic phenomena

Many empaths and HSP report paranormal experiences and psychic phenomenon. Some have seen spirits, heard spirit, can use their mind to heal others through visualisation and energy work. Keep a diary and make a note of any synchronicities (11:11, 22:22) or spiritual experiences.

A multifaceted approach is required, such as therapy as well as meditation, tarot cards - healthy coping mechanisms.

To open the third eye, one must practise; it meditation, exercise and have faith in something, regardless of religion. Many spiritual people believe in the Universe as a conscious being. If you are Muslim or Christian, it doesn't matter because the followers can still access the source through their faith.

Highly sensitive people and empaths are often drawn to the occult, and they seek answers and question things others don't. Many become self-taught in the areas of Tarot or Astrology to help answer their questions. Occult tools are fabulous methods for divination and problem solving, but they will only take you so far. The mind, body and spirit must be nourished and nurtured to really wield them as a tool and step into your power.

Recommended reading, films to watch to improve intuition and understanding of self, music, poetry, and art stirs your soul.

Consume media, music, art, anything that makes you emote. Notice what emotions stir and how it makes you feel. Do any memories appear? Writing this down in a journal can be beneficial.

I remember seeing a Michael Hussar painting for the first time; I was obsessed with it. It was so incredibly dark, weird, intriguing and confusing. I had never felt this way about a piece of art before. Similarly, psychological films pique my interest with the uncomfortable parts of myself. I have found it critical in my shadow work.

Intuition

You just know.

For some, it is a gut feeling. Some hear a voice, telling them. Many see images in both awake and dream states. This information can come in many different forms, it is up to you to find out what works. This is why meditation and being alone can aid psychic growth; most of us need silence and stillness to hear our higher selves. Not everything makes sense at the time, so if the intuition manifests, listen. In a world where emotions aren't openly accepted, it is courageous to listen to your inner self. Trusting the gut is essential!

Intuition is a sense. It requires trusting yourself, which can be difficult for individuals who had a difficult upbringing or experienced trauma. For people who have had such difficulties, it is imperative to build trust within.

Building inner trust requires you to speak kindly to yourself. Say you will do something and then action it, otherwise it is an empty promise to yourself. It is so much more than guessing numbers or colours, although those tasks help develop the psychic muscles.

Intuition and how it manifests in the body/mind

Intuition is a feeling. I feel negative intuition in my lower abdomen, it feels like a "pang" sensation, very sudden and usually when locking eyes with someone who isn't good for me. There are different types of intuition and these can be experienced differently amongst the psychic community. It is often deeply personal to us.

- A variety of people experience their intuition in the form of claircognizance - which is "divine knowing." At first, I found it extremely difficult to discern between divine knowing and my internal monologue. To me it sounds like a voice that is not quite my own, it appears and goes as quick as it came, and is usually not repeated.

- Clairaudience, where you hear divine information as if someone was whispering in your ear, or speaking to you as if they were in the room.
-
- Clairsentience, sensing and feeling. This trait is commonly seen in empaths. They walk into rooms and pick up the atmosphere. They experience shivers, goosebumps, body tingles and sensations in the body that can be deciphered.
-

- Clairvoyance tends to be visual, both in the minds' eye and in the physical realm, in the form of orbs, shadows, shimmering and seeing synchronicities such as angel numbers. They can have visions, vivid and prophetic dreams or interpret colours and other visual cues.

Some of us have gifts in all of these areas, some are particularly strong in one area. Which one doesn't matter: it is how we use these gifts positively, safely and to help others.

No one can tell you how to interpret and decipher your gift, but you can put knowledge from this ebook into practice and begin to develop yourself psychically. Seek out like-minded people in public places, HSP and Empaths tend to draw wounded people and attract toxic people. It is imperative to protect yourself and your energy!

Our bodies and energy

You may remember studying food chains in science at school. They show the flow of energy between species that consume one another. A dairy cow eats grass, the energy from the grass fuels the cow, which is integral to produce milk. Something will always become something else.

Start treating time as currency and see how much changes. Money is a man-made concept but time has always been there. See the difference? Our bodies can be drained of energy by people who do not have our best intentions at heart, toxic friends and family are still toxic. Tailor boundaries to match your needs. Some families maintain a low level of contact and manage to avoid inflammatory topics when they meet up and many of us had to remove ourselves from broken homes and dysfunctional relationships. You may need to seek help for this, which is common and recommended.

If you feel regenerated after time alone, it is highly likely that you possess traits of an HSP, Empath or both. Introversion gives us the time and space to work through our experiences and observations. This is a great time to write and create, channel these thoughts into a tangible, 3D object and see what comes up emotionally. This practice is vital for sensitive people and empaths.

Words have power as do thoughts

Words cast spells, that's why it's called spelling. Words can do harm, and they can be healing. ABRACADABRA - from old Hebrew, *"it will be created by my words"*, is used during stage magic performances. Its origins are arguably rooted in magick too. If we write out 'abracadabra' 11 times, all the letters match up diagonally.

A B R A C A D A B R A
A B R A C A D A B R
A B R A C A D A B
A B R A C A D A
A B R A C A D
A B R A C A
A B R A C
A B R A
A B R
A B
A

Notice the pattern here. It was once said that a person suffering with affliction should wear an amulet of the above to flush the disease out of the body, like a filter funnel.

When we witness someone spew vitriol, the atmosphere changes in the room. The negativity weighs heavily and then we carry that with us, often not knowing what to do with that experience. Many of us had difficulties at home or at school which created an internal critic, a part of our psyche that berates and tells us we are not good enough. This is internalised behaviour, something learned, and is therefore, not the truth. Speaking negatively internally or externally brings negativity. Like attracts like.

Negative thought patterns are difficult to break but it can be done. It requires patience and perseverance. Every positive affirmation and correction creates a neural pathway, which is called neuroplasticity. Hypnotherapy, EMDR, Neurofeedback therapies are fabulous for rewiring the brain with professional support, which is never anything to be ashamed of.

As the mind becomes more self-aware, kind and compassionate, the negative thought patterns neural pathway is used less and less, thus neuroplasticity has occurred. The new pathway allows us to be realistic and optimistic, instead of the perpetual misery we once knew.

I read somewhere that the first thought we have about someone is our prejudice. The second thought that follows, challenging the thought, shows who we really are. I still make snap judgments sometimes and this has been a pillar of support, knowing that I am continuously bettering myself and seeing others authentically, not what society projects.

Everyone wants to jump in and get going on honing their powers. Realistically, there is a lot of groundwork to be done. Psychological and emotional work will prepare you. Reality is not as it seems, and the mind must be open so it can manage the significant shifts that come with psychic powers. Humans can do incredible things: past lives, channelling, and mediumship are all common phenomena seen around the globe. You can tap into this too.

“Wake up, Neo”

In the cult classic, “The Matrix”, Neo is given clues from the universe that come in many different ways. His computer coding reveals he is looking for something but is unsure what. He has a good job, a warm home with a desktop computer, but still feels as though something is lacking. He plays by his own rules and ethics, which his company finds unsatisfactory. Trinity contacts him through his computer, telling him to follow the white rabbit. Neo’s door goes and the acquaintances invite him to a fetish club. He originally says no before spotting the white rabbit tattoo on one of the women in the group. Call it divine timing!

This is the universe preparing Neo for the information he is about to receive. The universe has sent Trinity to Neo, his divine feminine who wakes him up, by introducing him to Morpheus. Morpheus offers Neo the chance to see things for what they really are, and this is the information Neo has been seeking for so long, but the thought is terrifying. Morpheus offers to reveal all and break him free of the matrix, or he can learn it all but forget it in the morning. Neo chooses to break out and as soon as he makes this choice, the matrix tries to cling to him. Morpheus and the crew break Neo out of the matrix and he wakes in the farms. The human body is a generator which runs the machines. The human life force feeds them. It is a horrible sight.

Neo is so physically weak from the matrix, considering he has never actually "been" in his physical body, only the construct. "Why do my eyes hurt?" Neo asks. "You've never used them before," Morpheus answers.

Like Neo, people need time to adjust to their new environment and surroundings. It is incredibly difficult to break away from denial and truly open your eyes to the corruption and injustices in the world, realising that reality is far darker than once initially thought. But in the darkness is freedom, which is what we see from the crew on the "**NEBUCHADNEZZAR",** the ship from Zion in The Matrix. This is a biblical reference, which is unsurprising considering the entire franchise has layered metaphors and symbolism. Taken from "The Book of Daniel", it references enslavement, which translates to the humans being trapped in the matrix, feeding the machines with their biological energy.

Why are we discussing this film, you may ask? Well, like Neo, you too need time to integrate the learning so that you may adjust: "once you know, you cannot un-know."

Cypher is the character that regrets leaving the matrix and thinks "ignorance is bliss", thus causing mass destruction as he tries to attain that state through betrayal.

A spiritual awakening is not sunshine and butterflies. It can be the most heart-wrenching, eye-opening experience, and yes, like most things worth having, it comes as a result of hard work.

What does “hard work” mean, when working with spirituality? It means we must address everything that makes us, us. It requires deep introspection to peel back the layers and projections that society has pinned on us. We must question everything. It is tiring, and difficult to approach the “shadow” self, heal traumas and work on secure attachments, but it creates such a beautiful life.

First, we must address the physical body. Being present in the body - mindfulness of the feeling body. This is essentially being aware of the physical sensations in the body. Have you felt emotions in the body? Anger in the chest? That feeling similar to being hit in the stomach? It is all connected. Our emotions impact our physical and our physical being impacts our emotional and psychological being.

What does **your** intuition feel like? If you can’t feel it yet, this preparation step is vital.

Tools and exercises to support you:

- Trauma release exercises such as: somatic experiencing, EMDR, EFT Tapping, myofascial release (foam rolling, GuaSha scraping, acupuncture, cupping) - anything that helps remove emotional trauma from the body, usually from the muscles

- Sensory deprivation
- Sea salt baths (Epsom)
- Reiki/massage
- Listening and adhering to body needs such as hunger, thirst, tiredness
- Yoga and exercise
- Sensory stimulation for grounding - creating art/music/food
- Singing and managing breath, also known as grounding.

Meditation is probably one of the most difficult things to master because many people think it is about sitting still for hours on end. This is just one way to practice meditation. It is not a one size fits all approach. As a neurodiverse person, I tend to find my mindfulness comes when I am painting. I am able to identify my thoughts and feelings, unconscious bias and judgements come to the surface, old wounds and traumatic memories appear and sometimes I am interrupted by intrusive thoughts. You are not alone. Being mindful is not about having an “empty mind" but rather the ability to observe your thoughts and feelings.

If you are someone who is bombarded with intrusive thoughts, my hypnotherapist gave me a great visualisation technique: imagine the intrusive thoughts as random people walking past you on the street, beach, wherever. Don’t engage them, just acknowledge their presence. The more we try to ignore negative thoughts, feelings or intrusive thoughts, the more they appear. Like the mythical Hydra, cut off one head and two return in its place. Acknowledge, accept, let go.

The longest relationship we have is the one with yourself. There are five love languages: words of affirmation, acts of service, quality time, physical touch and receiving gifts. How do you show love? How do you like to receive love? What type of love did you experience from your caregivers? These are vital points that can bring up a lot of old wounds and traumas. However, this is a fabulous way to align yourself and identify when your needs aren't being met. You can take the love language test online for free.

By observing our behaviours and reactions, we begin to understand that everyone is fighting a battle of their own. Human behaviour forms patterns and patterns can be predicted. We begin to see the insidiousness of society and can often pinpoint the day we lost our childhood. Being able to empathise with hurt and wounded people is a blessing and a curse, the latter only if you do not set boundaries and negate spiritual protection.

Equally, being self-aware points a spotlight to mental health struggles and illness, and many identify with conditions stated in the DSM-V. This handbook ridiculously rejected Complex PTSD (childhood trauma, interpersonal relationship trauma for example) much to the disdain of Dr Bessel Van Der Kolk, author of "The Body Keeps the Score." This book is a pillar of support for so many on their healing journeys. Dr Bessel is a veteran psychiatrist who has tried and tested many therapies, taking new and innovative trauma approaches back to his practice. In his book, there are so many pieces of anecdotal evidence, a real breadth and depth of traumas from real people, and their stories told so delicately. It was one of the most amazing and difficult books I have ever read.

Trauma survivors often have a dysregulated nervous system, which famously presents as PTSD. Jumping at sudden noises, flinching when touched, sweating profusely, nightmares, dissociation, flashbacks which can be visual, emotional (feeling), auditory, physical or psychological which can manifest as a psychotic break, usually brought on by a large stressor. Identifying triggers and finding their root cause can be difficult and I encourage everyone to seek help where necessary. Please, please reach out if you are struggling. You were placed on this planet for a reason.

All of the above can take varying lengths of time to achieve, sometimes, decades. Comparison is the thief of joy, try and stay focussed on your journey. Stop and smell the roses along the way.

Empaths and highly sensitive people in childhood

These individuals often experience childhood trauma or difficulties when growing up due to their sensitivities. Many become more empathetic and sensitive as the result of dysfunction during the formative years. Attachment theory is used to describe the connection we have with our care-givers during our formative years, usually with a mother or father. Regardless of the family dynamic, every human has an attachment style. A lot of children were left 'to cry it out' and this method was actively encouraged, which has negatively influenced parent-child dynamics for up to 2-3 generations. We are now aware due to experiments such as the 'flat face effect' how much children rely on our social cues and us as adults, to provide care and nurture. Many children cannot self soothe until highschool, it really depends on their lived experience and relationships at home.

Nuclear Family Roles and Dysfunction

The term "nuclear family" describes a heteronormative, married couple with children. Fortunately, LGBTQIA+ families are becoming more common, especially as countries open up adoption to queer parents.

There are common family dynamics that individuals fall into, some terms you may already be familiar with are: golden child, scapegoat, parentified child, hero, clown and the rescuer/caretaker. These roles appear when there is codependency, family enmeshment, abuse, bereavements and so on. It shows there is an imbalance in family relationships.

Attachment theory

Attachment is a biological function. It bonds a mother and child, and research shows that any parent, regardless of gender, can form an intense attachment to their child. A secure attachment is when the child and parent have healthy boundaries, spend quality time together, make efforts to understand and educate each other and for the parent to provide emotional support and guidance as they age. When this is not present, it is so incredibly damaging to a persons' psyche. They internalise their parents' issues and then create core beliefs around them, such as: "I'm only good enough when I help mum" or "my emotions are too much because I am more sensitive than my peers." Attachment continues into our adult lives, replayed out in relationships often with surrogates to play the roles of the adults in our childhood. Trauma and poor attachment block intuition because we are not at one with ourselves. Repression and suppression are blockages that prevent authenticity.

Neurotypes

Undiagnosed neurodiversity in the form of autism, ADHD, dyslexia and epilepsy, for example are all differences in neurotype. These brains are wired differently from neurotypical people and even have differences from other divergent neurotypes. Autistic children in particular can be susceptible to their environments, experiencing sensory difficulties which can be exacerbated by psychic phenomena. This was true for me. I eventually closed down my psychic gifts because I had a frightening experience and was also incredibly overwhelmed with my family dysfunction, struggles at school and difficulties with interpersonal relationships. Communication for some autistics and ADHD folk can be challenging, so improving their intuition and telepathy skills will provide support—many people who are neurodiverse report psychic phenomena and identify as profoundly empathetic. *As a scientist, I believe there is an overlap here amongst neurotypes and psychic gifts.*

Learned behaviour and Trauma Bonding

Our dysfunctional patterns learned in childhood cause us to play out the same dynamics in our adult lives. We emulate our relationships that our parents had with us and each other, thus perpetuating a cycle. A child who breaks out of a dysfunctional dynamic is usually estranged from their family, known as a "black sheep."

Our brains are wired to find the path of least resistance and neural pathways are created by our thought patterns. If we consistently experience abuse or mistreatment, it becomes innate to the person because it is all they know; they do not have any other neural pathways yet to take them out of this cycle.

Therapy, particularly hypnotherapy and neurofeedback, are great therapies to promote neuroplasticity. Winning against negativity is so much more than "just being positive." A trauma bond is where two people have a shared experience and become bonded through this.

For example, Stockholm Syndrome is where a relationship forms as a result of captivity, as seen in Beauty and the Beast, where Belle starts as a prisoner then becomes his lover. There is a considerable influx of neurotransmitters and hormone rush associated with trauma bonding, which is why it makes it so challenging to leave abusive situations. The brain is addicted to its chemicals, stimulated by this person's behaviours and actions.

Empaths and relationships

An awakened empath seeks an emotionally available partner, knows their worth and sets boundaries to manage their energy levels. Prior to awakening, many empaths go through difficult and even abusive relationships.

The difficult relationships usually begin at home due to insecure attachment issues or a sensitive child being raised in an abusive environment. These patterns tend to repeat themselves at school, where the child can end up a victim of bullying if they are particularly emotional or introverted. As they mature, the empaths become teenagers and adults who struggle with self-esteem and boundaries, due to not experiencing secure love.

Empaths and sensitive people can end up with partners who are: energy vampires, co-dependent or commonly, narcissists. They tend to unconsciously seek partners with insecure attachment styles until they become aware of the things that caused this programming and actively try to heal.

These relationships will leave empaths exhausted and often, mentally ill, due to abuse and gaslighting. Their nervous systems are always on edge, and they can no longer discern intuition or gut feelings. Empaths eventually have a Tower moment - an important card in Tarot - where they realise they deserve better, and find the path back to themselves. This is why shadow work and therapy is integral, not only for healing, but for having a fulfilled life as a sensitive person.

Empaths and careers

As we know, empathetic people are susceptible to overwhelm. It can be really difficult to find and hold down a job in this current climate, but also due to the job not being in alignment with you. Some of us are unfortunately forced to work jobs we don't want or dislike but are required to as we need the money. Some of us have dependents and there is no other choice but to work at this job. Other chapters in the book can help with this for people who are struggling, but the main point here is to guide our young people into careers that feed their souls and protect their energy; they should not become participants of the rat race. It breeds unhappiness and disquiet, let them be their authentic selves and innovate. Listen to them! Fresh new ideas are exactly what are needed!

We need more counsellors, Montessori teachers, trauma informed practitioners in the military, schools, prisons, yoga studios - everywhere! We really need empathetic and compassionate people in these specific areas of society, to help our future generations deal with the emotional and psychological impact of an unstable government, wars and a pandemic.

Jobs to be avoided: working with the general public in retail or hospitality, complaints departments.

Empath self-care

Sensitive people and empaths must take care of themselves. Their energy levels are prone to wild variations, where it peaks and troughs, leaving them very drained. They must set strong boundaries and be strict with how much time they spend with certain individuals. If an empath loves you, they will set boundaries to help maintain a healthy relationship with you. Empaths require a lot of solitude, so make sure people know your schedule.

This is important because it lets friends and family know when you are available and for how long. It doesn't have to be awkward if you make your limits known prior to an event. Only you can keep your cup full. Forget what other people think! If you do not want to go to a party, say no straight away and say there is a prior engagement, even if that engagement is you watching TV in your PJs!

Cleansing energy and space after having people over or hanging around with friends and family is essential to maintain balance. Get the windows cracked open and the incense out to cleanse your space.

Wearing protective jewelry such as obsidian/tourmaline crystals will repel and transmute any negative energies moving towards you. Crystals can be worn as rings, earrings and necklaces for their many uses, which will be discussed in a later chapter.

Reading self-help books, attending therapy, reaching out to communities for support are key factors in an empaths self-care tool kit. They need a support system that is multifaceted because they feel so much, it can be difficult to make sense of.

Looking after a pet or having an animal at home is very comforting. Petting a dog, cat or rabbit has been proven to lower blood pressure and bring the nervous system into balance. We also make strong links with our furry family members, who often love to snuggle up on the couch with us. We release endorphins such as oxytocin and dopamine which then help us bond. Dogs in particular can read human faces and are quite expressive themselves. Alternative pets generally require lots of research and specific habitats, possibly specific dietary requirements too. This is a good option for someone who is meticulous and has a routine in place. Snakes and spiders have different rest periods between meals in comparison to mammals. Taking care of them can evoke the same response in individuals and these creatures are capable of being gentle if you are.

Jungian Psychology

Dr Carl Jung was a Swiss Psychologist and Psychiatrist, known for his theories on the dark aspects of the psyche. Dr Jung is truly a pioneer in analytical psychology, and many spiritualists resonate with this approach in particular.

As a child, Carl experienced a lonely childhood but was enriched by observing adult relationships. Carl also saw his mother with spirit; he was not blind to psychic phenomena. He also experienced trauma in childhood. His family were both religious and spiritual, his mothers' side being the latter.

Upon his childhood experiences and parental relationships, Dr Jung coined the term "complex", where based on a common theme, there is an association. A conglomeration of emotionally charged concepts, triggers, associations, memories, become complexes. For example, a child who grew up in a cold, critical environment tends to grow up with a primary inferiority complex, directly caused as a result of an abusive environment and insecure attachment.

Firstly, let's break down the Jungian approach to the human psyche.

The psyche contains all psychological processes. Narnia was hidden in a wardrobe; we too have a fantasy world locked away inside. We have different aspects to our personality which each have a function. Like everything, there are positive and negative aspects appointed to the subsections of the psyche.

Persona

The persona is our outward personality. For most, this can be a mask or a costume to hide who they really are. Sometimes we have to play a role in order to survive, but when the time comes to discard that role, it can be very upsetting when you realise you don't know who you are. The positive thing about this is, you are now able to curate and decide who you want to be.

Ego

The ego ties into the persona aspect and influences our behaviour. It marries the unconscious and conscious thoughts, questions reality and describes self-identity. Some survivors may have a core belief that they are not good enough, their self esteem is low and therefore their ego can become gigantic. Think of Lord Farquaad from Shrek, a very insecure man who tortured fairy-tale creatures! A balanced ego can identify a persons' strengths and weaknesses, turning them into actions and growth.

Ego Death

The ego may have infinite layers, and we must move to shed them all.

An ego death causes radical change within oneself and can be caused by life-changing experiences and psychedelics.

When we work through an ego death, we are working to be left with the awareness and detachment, our only "job" or purpose, is to exist. Now, this can feel like death.

Think about where you have felt emotions in the body. I am confident that most of you have experienced that heart-wrenching chest pain, the absolute agony that ripples through the cavity and the ribs. This is the pain of sadness, grief, regret, many solemn and distressing emotions bundled inside.

That gut drop when you see someone you are falling for, or even in love with, with someone else. It's the drop kick feeling to the stomach that you almost wish someone hit you, instead of having to feel the emotional pain.

An ego death can feel like this.

It can also be a scary experience when using psychedelics if you are not in alignment with your mind. An ego death can also present as a temporary loss of self, some folk lost the ability to speak their native language or their sober sitter couldn't comprehend the gibberish being spoken. Either way, a temporary loss in some aspect of the psyche is typical. Sometimes the gap remains and sometimes that gap is the space for something new to come in.

In 1943, the scientist Albert Hoffmann accidentally consumed lysergic acid diethylamide (LSD) whilst working on a chemical vasoconstrictor (a drug that constricts the blood vessels). He noted the effects and tried a larger dose, which he had assumed was still relatively low. He was wrong. He had a three day trip and famously cycled his bicycle home tripping and had an outer body experience whilst on his couch.

Hoffman felt great after the experience and considered its use in psychiatry. It was adopted in the practice where he worked and was taken on by British scientists who noted its efficacy in treating addiction. In the late 1960s, politicians became fearful of its powerful effects which then led into the Nixon led war on drugs - this was actually a war on progressives wanting to end segregation between white people and people of colour. More on this later.

Eckharte Tolle spoke about the “ego identity and the path to inner peace.” During this keynote speech, he stated that humans have the “dimension of consciousness”, which differs from the rest. This is a spiritual awakening and is the next step in human evolution. We are not the finished product by any means. He muses, how awful it would be if this was it, the final form of human evolution. He refers to a deeper state of consciousness that stands alone from the personal hurts, traumas, social conditionings and your personality.

Many humans are trapped on the surface area of reality, trapped in their physical form and psychologically through social programming. Eckharte spoke about “normal people being insane.” However, he is also aware that the spiritual ego can create a level of superiority, which is why the ego must be shed in layers.

“Who am I?” The ego hides behind I and Me statements.

Shadow

The shadow is the aspect of our psyche that has a bad reputation and people assume it is scary. Like the dark side of the moon, people fear what they cannot see and assume some evil shenanigans are afoot. Again, this is not true.

Shadow work has to be one of the most life changing experiences ever. Once you accept the light and dark within has nothing to do with good or evil, it becomes far easier to identify when the shadow can come out and be applied. There are aspects of our shadow that are protective in nature. The shadow self holds creativity and chaos, but if it is not integrated, reap and sow negativity.

"*Knowing your own darkness is the best method for dealing with the darknesses in other people*" - Dr Carl Jung

The shadow is the opposite of the ego image. The ego tends to reject the shadow and denies the existence of the shadow qualities of their own personality. Denial becomes repressed emotions and memories, the shadow becomes larger. As previously mentioned, the shadow aspect is nothing to fear, it is you. Love this shadow, accept your shadow and acknowledge when the shadow's skills are required.

- Use shadow work to remove things that no longer serve you, such as; behaviours, addictions, judging others
- Transform and transmute anger and grief (feel the feelings, explore the root cause, then turn them into something powerful). Grief brings the opportunity to be empathetic to others.
- Knowing your shadow, traumas, triggers and wounds manages the behaviour and energy sent out to the world, in a positive manner. Integration of the shadow allows you to observe yourself and others from a higher view, emotionally detached so it doesn't harm your peace but still connected to provide empathy.

"Every person must choose how much truth they can stand" - Dr Carl Jung

Once we know something, we cannot unknow it. This makes shadow work very difficult for some people as the pain is too much to bear, this often presents as denial.

Anima/Animus

The masculine and feminine aspects of the psyche are known as the Animus and Anima, respectively. This does not equate to biological gender, but rather the primordial forces within us seen throughout time. Adam and Eve, Morticia and Gomez, these archetypes have been seen across indigenous communities and religions.

The Anima (masculine) is responsible for the following in a healthy person, who in this example is biologically female.

"Every man carries within him the eternal image of woman, not the image of this or that particular woman, but a definite feminine image. This image is fundamentally unconscious, a hereditary factor of primordial origin engraved in the living organic system of the man, an imprint or "archetype" of all the ancestral experiences of the female, a deposit, as it were, of all the impressions ever made by woman-in short, an inherited system of psychic adaptation. Even if no women existed, it would still be possible, at any given time, to deduce from this unconscious image exactly how a woman would have to be constituted psychically. The same is true of the woman: she too has her inborn image of man."

- Dr Carl Jung, a passage from "Marriage as a psychological relationship".

"Marriage as a Psychological Relationship" (1925) In CW 17: The Development of the Personality. P.338

A great example of the animus being present in a female, is when a woman takes her dog for a walk. She knows the route they are taking, time it will take and any items required for their walk will be organised. When the woman leads with her innate anima, the dog walk would be intuitively led by her animal, with no time constraints and lots of stopping to smell the roses.

At our very core, we are human beings. Our souls are energy. This physical body is our vessel and can be expressed in any way you desire. If you do not resonate with the gender binary, consider approaching the anima and animus as yin and yang. They imply duality and balance is always needed.

When two adults meet who have integrated psyches, work on their shadow and balanced internal anima/animu, they can create an incredible relationship that transcends gender roles. Men need to be held and brought flowers, just as women need to feel powerful. Embracing and supporting each other outwith the realms of society shows us that love is love. Discard anything else.
Self

Dr Jung proposed 12 archetypes of the self that describe the basic human range of motivation. Jung was heavily influenced by his psychic and mythological experiences. They are: The Innocent, Everyman, Hero, Outlaw, Explorer, Creator, Ruler, Magician, Lover, Caregiver, Jester, and Sage.

Each archetype is looking for satisfaction in the following:

- Ego – Leave their legacy and make their mark
- Order – Provide a structure to the world
- Social – Create and maintain human connection
- Freedom – Seek paradise

The Caregiver

- Love thy neighbour as yourself
- Core desire: to protect and care for others
- Core belief: to help others
- Repulsed by: selfishness and ingratitude
- Strategy for success: doing things for others
- Wounds: martyrdom and exploitation
- Traits: compassion, generosity, patience, good listening skills

Also known as: The saint, altruist, parent, helper, supporter.

The following discusses the shadow aspects of this archetype. A person will have a "self' archetype, which comes with shadow aspects too. Caregivers can find themselves as a: codependent, victim and slave.

Codependency with a caregiver archetype can turn incredibly toxic. They end up pouring from an empty cup. They show love outwardly and their main love language tends to be acts of service and words of affirmation. This can further turn into a power dynamic where they become a victim in their relationships, as they are psychologically wired to care for another person, even to their own detriment. We see this finalised in the slave aspect, where the caregiver gives all of themselves and resentment settles in.

These archetypes became the blueprint for the MBTI Myers-Briggs Personality test. Jung also proposed introversion and extroversion, which heavily influences how personality traits are projected, how, when and why.

https://www.myersbriggs.org/my-mbti-personality-type/mbti-basics/

Our true self is a mix of archetypes, with different abilities. https://www.mbtionline.com describes what is being measured:

“How you get your energy (Extraversion vs. Introversion)

How you take in information and learn (Sensing vs. Intuition)

How you make decisions (Thinking vs. Feeling)
How you like to organize your time and environment (Judging vs. Perceiving)

INF and ENF - (INFJ, ENFJ, ISFP for example) any F* types are known to be the most empathetic, caring and compassionate.”

A healthy, integrated self no longer seeks to conform. This individual seeks their own happiness and acts accordingly to achieve their goals. They are self-aware and actively work on shadow aspects that can get triggered by our experiences in life. There is also a healthy balance of the ego, which manifests as humble confidence, but is also a vein that can be tapped into. We often see this in drag performers, actors and even Beyonce, her alter ego being Sasha Fierce.

Our psyche is affected by learned behaviours in childhood, which we discussed earlier. However, it is also deeply impacted by sexual trauma, in the form of repression.

When we deny our true sexual self, we remove the space for creation. Our creativeness comes from our sacral chakra, the womb space. If our sexuality and desires are not embraced or welcomed, how can we truly be ourselves? Sexual assault, familial shame, cultural shame, homophobia, transphobia, religious shame, the list is very long. The word “libido” does not only refer to sexual energy, but to psychic energy in general. When we repress our true sexual selves, we will find it incredibly difficult to heal our shadow aspects. Whoever you are, whatever you identify as or pursue sexually/romantically, is valid. Other people's homophobia, for example, is usually the result of a psychological complex or the repression of this person’s true nature.

To integrate your true nature, recognise your uniqueness.

Jung vs Freud

Jung and Freud did originally hypothesise and debate together, but eventually branched off into two separate schools of psychoanalysis. Essentially, Freud thought that the destination is the goal, whereas Jung felt it was the journey not the destination, that relates to the meaning of life.

Freudian theories are also deeply sexual in nature, known as “psychosexual.” He believed behaviour is rooted in sexual urges, whereas Jung theorised sexuality and impulse is not as pressing in regards to behaviour.

Divine Sex practices and Sexual Healing

Demetra George's book, "Mysteries of the Dark Moon" discusses the divine goddesses' approach to sexual intercourse. Before the patriarchal religions took over, feminine, goddess worship was the blueprint. The divine feminine could have sex before marriage and this was encouraged so that she would be prepared for her wifely duties as well as experience the divine masculine, inviting him to her temple. For women in this era, sex was not sinful or dirty. Young women would work as priestesses in temples, caring for the weary and being in tune with their sexual, giving nature. It was the patriarchal gaze who tainted this practice in sin, adding shame. True sexual intimacy brings about the "Kundalini Awakening" and asks you to integrate your divine sexual nature. Sexual experiences are to be long, drawn-out, sensual experiences, designed to give and receive love, affection and attention from your sexual partner.

Like the archetypes of personality, this also applies to the divine feminine, in the act of sex. There are sacred prostitute archetypes, positive attitudes to sex workers, who provide human connection. This also derives from Jungian psychology.

Sex was considered a divine union that had healing and manifestation properties, outside of reproduction. Again, the feminine archetypes have been observed through each era of human existence in deities and goddesses such as: Isis, Orishas, Aphrodite, Diana, Helen of Troy and unsurprisingly, Mary Magdalene.

The goddesses led the way by using the moon cycles as the blueprint. The farmers' almanac follows the seasons and lunar cycles to reap and sow. The first-ever calendar was written on the surface of a femur bone, anthropologists believe it was an attempt at tracking the menstrual cycle.

The Maiden, The Mother, The Crone, are metaphors for the stage in a woman's life, and also that of the lunar phases. The cycle of death and rebirth is reflected in the moon, the menstrual cycle, the seasons and our experiences. If nothing ends, how do things begin?

Mary Magdalene was described by the bible as a prostitute, who needed salvation from the lord and saviour Jesus Christ. This patriarchal gaze sought to degrade her and deemed her association to Jesus about repentance for her flagrant sexuality. In reality, Mary Magdalene was a priestess who had embraced the animus and identified the injustices in society, towards Jesus, who was her counterpart in the divine masculine. Unawakened men saw his love and acceptance as weakness, and his empathy for the poor disgusted those in power. This dynamic has not changed during the patriarchal rule. We still have the Donald Trumps, Vladimir Putins and Kim Jong Uns of the world, trying to shout about who's got the biggest dick, or in this case, nuclear weapons.

Divine female archetypes: the Maiden, the Mother, the Huntress, the Wise Woman, the Wild Woman (or Mystic), and the Queen.

The wild woman archetype depicts a certain sexual nature. This woman is magic incarnate. We could roam the woods naked and barefoot or walk into a palace and assume the throne. She is deeply in tune with her intuition, wants and needs. This woman seeks solitude and it is essential to her health and wish fulfilment. When this archetype is at odds or unbalanced, it presents as chaotic, destructive, unpredictable behaviours. She is a storm and feels her emotions deeply.

Again, to find out what archetype you are, there are lots of free resources online.

Female Pleasure

Female pleasure is powerful. Not many people know that the climax of orgasm is an optimum moment for manifestation. Whether you are loving yourself or with a partner, ask the universe for what you desire and let the wonderful vibrations of orgasm lift you higher. The universe is happy when you feel happy, satiated and pleasured. The yoni is a portal. It is the organ of transformation, bleeding and transforming a girl to a woman, accepting and receiving penetration, divine union through sex, and finally, the incredible act of childbirth. The clitoris has more nerve endings than the head of the penis. It is a large sex organ that requires delicate attention, which will unravel a beautiful flower. The divine masculine knows there is no greater achievement than making his divine female experience an earth-shattering orgasm. He is focused on his enthusiastic participation and her enjoyment. In return, the divine feminine let go, penetrated, mind, body and soul.

Sex energy exchange - the best time for manifestation is orgasm

Believe it or not, when we climax in the physical world, it spurs energy into our deepest desires and manifestations, this is actually a great way to charge your intentions. New moons in particular are powerful manifestors, so, maybe some sex magick could be on the cards?

Whatever your sexuality, whether you are able-bodied or have a disability, none of that matters when it comes to sex. If you have two consenting, of age partners who are willing to communicate - then what does it matter? Remove the shame that society projects.

Masturbation is not evil. It is a healthy practice that grounds the mind into the body. You must be physically present to orgasm. When feeling emotionally charged, it can help take the edge off. It is always recommended that before going on a date, you masturbate beforehand to avoid being blinded by lust. It is a very mature way of approaching a date or potential partner, it encourages you to stay in your lane until there is expressed consent from the other party.

It has also been scientifically proven to flood the brain with endorphins, feel good chemicals such as dopamine, serotonin and oxytocin (the bonding hormone) bring a natural high with lots of great physical attributes such as: lowering cortisol and adrenaline therefore allowing the nervous system to relax, lowered blood pressure, increased bonding - if with a partner(s) - post-orgasm sleep, increased appetite and wish to nourish the body, feeling present and mindful, sexy and deserving.

Again, the projection of sin may have began from original western Abrahamic religions - Islam and Judaism but is also rampant in the many forms of christianity, which was born from Judiaism. Female pleasure is innately powerful and is feared. The Torah tells a story of a man who is dying, but a woman will make him feel better. The Rabbi tells his Dr, the woman is not required to do anything for a man, even if he is dying. Noone is entitled to a woman, regardless of the circumstances.

Catholicism as a religion carries a lot of shame. This may be hard to hear for people with roots in catholicism, but hear me out. The acts of sex are considered shameful, knowing about the human body - shameful, aborting a child for a myriad of reasons - shameful. However, the insidious abuse from catholic church continues to go unchecked. The depth of abuse has never truly been uncovered, and never will be for as long as women are at the forefront of the religion, having the finger pointed at them.

There were churches in Ireland where young mothers and prostitutes were sent, who had a baby out of wedlock. These women were so badly abused, which can be seen in the film by Peter Mullen, 'The Magdalene Sisters' which is an incredibly violent and accurate display of what happened inside the institutions. Many of these women were raped by men and fell pregnant, were sent to Magdalene Asylums and forced into heavy labour. In 1993, a mass grave in Dublin was found, which led the Irish government to pay reparations, however, there has never been a full investigation as the government feels that lies outside their remit. This is why I believe church and state must always be two separate things, so one cannot influence the other.

Sexual Healing

Empathetic people, highly sensitive people, and those with disabilities tend to be more vulnerable to sexual assault and abuse. Autistic women are far more likely to experience trauma than neurotypicals, depending on the individuals' social abilities as autism is a divergence in how humans communicate. Many are naive and can be taken advantage of.

So if you are apart of the 1 in 4 who experienced a sexual assault, let me tell you: it was not your fault. Their shadow, ego, projections, traumas and wounds overpowered them. They will have the intense karmic debt of a thousand suns and you will burn for eternity. Reclaim your sexual power. Say it out loud. Say it every day, remember words create reality. You are a goddess, you are healing and you have all the power, even when you don't feel like it. Remember who you are.

The moon circles the earth and the full lunar cycle takes 29 days. The menstruation cycle tends to last around 28 days. Some women menstruate at the full moon, making them a "red moon woman", or bleeding at the new moon makes a "white moon woman." There are also pink and purple cycles, for the waxing and waning phases of the moon.

Menstruation is a part of sexual healing. Acknowledging the body and its needs (such as extra calories during the period), the need to rest, feel and be present in your emotions. When we deny our menstrual needs, Demetra George said that our unconscious views skew our needs. There is a stigma of shame related to the menstrual cycle. It is always a big secret, no one should know and no person should see, especially not a man, god forbid. This ridiculous notion that menses is dirty or wrong, is again the result of a patriarchal view, and incorrect translation of cultural practices. Many women stayed in a different area, not because they were bad or wrong, but because they needed rest and isolation from the rest of the tribe. We can see how deeply and badly affected people can be from the physical aspect of menstruation, it is absolutely valid to want to retreat from relationships and responsibilities. This is also a great time to practice some magick!

The four phases are: (remember not everyone syncs up like this, don't panic)

Menstrual (New Moon): Rest, reflect and set intentions
Follicular (Waxing Moon): Begin taking action, initiate creative projects
Ovulation (Full Moon): Present, be in front of people, collaborate. Shine.
Luteal (Waning Moon): Complete tasks, stay focused, finish projects
https://highbrowhippie.com/blogs/highbrow-hippie-blog/go-with-the-flow

In many cultures and in astrology, the Moon is known as the divine feminine. La Luna is a mysterious being, dark sometimes and illuminating the other times. She too waxes and wanes like the female womb. The divine masculine is represented by the sun.

The sacral chakra is tied to the womb, and the womb is the source of all creation. Irrespective of gender, you can tap into the sacral chakra and channel this power. Opening and closing chakras will be discussed later in this ebook. Since this is the source of creativity, wouldn't sex dampen this? NO!

The patriarchal view deemed sex as sinful and immoral when in fact, divine intercourse between two loving and consenting folks is the closest we can get to the source. It is our most primal act, born at the dawn of time. If this was not meant to be, then why does the human brain have a chemical cascade system, based entirely on human interaction and sexual intercourse? Other mammals mate as and when for biological reproduction and some mate for life. Animals are sentient beings and too, release hormones as a result of human stimulus.

Mating for life is a concept (not set in stone) because being sexually compatible isn't always something to be taught. If there is a connection, it is incredibly difficult to fake. You will feel this connection in your mind, body and soul, so imagine how this will feel when it's time for divine intercourse! If you do choose to be monogamous, communication is key. Marriage is another option, but this is not, and should not, be the blueprint for relationships.

Divine masculine reading this, it is your job to correct straight men who disrespect women and others in this manner. You have the power and the initiative to influence and change others. Lead by example, model the proper way to treat people and challenge the misogyny around you. The patriarchy hurts men. It literally aids the few, who are the white, straight, elite men we currently have in power.

Men will suffer from their mental health when their divine feminine is overpowering them and will be domineering and aggressive when the masculine is driving them. We see severe acts of violence all the time. We see suicides from young men on the news daily. It is time to protect one another and start sexual healing.

Sexual healing can come in many forms, but please ensure you obtain the help of a licensed practitioner, should you seek someone out for:

- yoni massage
- safe yoni steaming (cultural practices and some people may be too sensitive to receive this treatment, which can throw out the natural pH of the vagina and vulva inducing a yeast infection
- sex therapy

- **Porn and low vibrational sex**

- I am not going to engage the negative here, we already know the damage that mainstream porn has done. Addiction and instant sexual gratification play a huge part in the porn culture we see today.

- Please consider engaging in ethical porn, where the actors are paid royalties, there are diverse storylines and people, it has been created with morality in mind. Even amateur porn with real-life consenting couples is a good start because it is all about human connection.

- I'm sure, regardless of gender and sexuality, that many folk have experienced really rubbish sex. There are some selfish lovers out there who only wish to take from you. Avoid them like the plague.

- Guide for higher consciousness sex

- So you have a special someone, you are both consenting, ready and willing to have sex. Why not make a ritual out of it? Set your intentions for the intimate act together beforehand: what do you want to achieve? Are there any boundaries? What things are you trying to manifest? Are you willing to cleanse spiritually and physically before our union?

- Energy can attach to us, so it is essential we remove all negative energies attached to us and our partner, prior to penetration, as this act is a transfer of energy. We don't want to take on something that is not ours.

- Sex Magick

- Light candles, call for protection, get physical protection and continue to check in with your partner before, during and after. Don't forget to journal, watch out for your manifestations appearing! You may need:
    - Candles
    - Condoms and lubrication - regardless of gender, please make sure you have the necessary tools for safe and enjoyable sex. Many people regardless of age require lubrication, particularly partners that practice anal sex. For AFAB, diaphragms and mouth condoms are a good option. I would also encourage all parties involved to have a STI health check prior to sleeping together.
    - Drinks and snacks
    - Warmth (bedding/blankets)
    - Journal
    - Crystals
    - Dried flowers

Using the above ingredients as part of a ritual can make the sexual experience more intense and pleasant, as you are actively putting time and effort, which is required for large manifestations. Rarely will someone wake up with a business plan in their lap, ready to go and churning out millions of profit from the get-go. No, some things require more effort and more gratitude - and that is perfectly in line with the universe.

By creating a ritual, you are taking things seriously. You are able to clearly articulate your intentions and manifest them through consensual sex with a chosen partner. What a lovely way to manifest!

Please remember that the sex scenes we see on TV and in porn do not reflect typical daily experiences. Sex can be funny and awkward, and the best way to navigate this is through communication.

Chapter Two

If you have recently gone through a spiritual awakening, or are currently in a difficult place, this chapter is for you. In this chapter you will learn how to master your mind, which is exactly the reason I am putting this technique before the explanation of the Dark Night is to provide a coping mechanism or a point of resonance for people who have experienced this. The tool I am about to explain is used amongst therapists and individuals to manage inner child work and voices that people hear internally. Hearing "parts" is very common and is a great therapy tool for those who have an internal monologue. I taught myself "Internal Family System" but please bear in mind, I have done a lot of work to get to the point where I could handle IFS. IFS is where you identify if:

- Repressed and hidden parts of your personality, can be from childhood so do not be alarmed if you are hearing yourself as a child, it's very commonly known as "The Inner Child"
- Parts of yourself that took the brunt of the issue/trauma/abuse and find it difficult to step back even though the 'threat' has gone.

- Calling on parts of you for certain jobs or skills - drag personas, acting are great examples
- Highlights social perspectives and pressures, sometimes even the year you took them on (particular body shaming or starting drinking to fit in)

As a result, I started talking to myself internally, properly and without fear that I was insane. I began to re-parent myself, tell myself when I was proud of my achievements, and acknowledge when I was standing in my own way because I was being triggered by old wounds. This is how I picked myself back up and dusted myself off. I didn't think I would come out of 2020 alive and well, never mind surviving and thriving. We all have a purpose and I'm glad you're here too!

It is the sheer loss, pain and grief that accelerates a spiritual awakening because you are now able to empathise with everything and everyone. Compassion flows freely and we understand that pain is universal, but so is kindness. If you have ever been at rock bottom, and someone treated you like shit at a time you needed kindness, love, empathy, support - you internalise it, and promise to never do someone like that. Moving through life with compassion for others makes it so much easier to navigate. If you think about how much internal worries, woes and thoughts go on in your own mind, it must be the same for others right? Having this knowledge allows a higher view, an emotionally detached perspective allows you to identify core beliefs.

St John of the Cross wrote a poem, Noche Oscura, about the dark night of the soul. Scott F. Fitzgerald was inspired to write about "the long dark night of the soul." It has been referenced throughout history by many and often is expressed through some form of artistry.

The exit of the dark night of the soul usually brings a new, invigorated sense of life. Some may have found religion, sobriety, clarity and some go on to help others by starting to volunteer, do charity work or create a sanctuary for animals. They realised that we are all one and we all experience life differently. Some of us need a little extra help and compassion, and that is ok.

But what exactly is it?

Another term is a "spiritual awakening." In Jungian psychology, we discussed the ego. For true compassion and integration of all aspects of self, the ego has to die, or at least, get knocked down a peg!

Metaphysician Ananda Coomaraswamy said, "no creature can attain a higher grade of nature without ceasing to exist." A great example of this is the metamorphosis of the butterfly. The caterpillar becomes goo, inside a cocoon, and emerges as this gorgeous creature that can fly! However, they are vulnerable upon exiting their cocoon as their wings must dry out in the sun before their first flight. I believe this to be the reflection stage, just before you re-integrate to society with what you've learned, and a plan for yourself.

How to recognise it:

- Relationships and friendships falling apart – breakups, fallouts, miscommunications, gossip, feeling left out or purposely alienated
- Actively seeking isolation after the above experiences because human interaction and interpersonal relationships become increasingly difficult
- Denial and Anxiety; there has to be more to life than this? What if there isn't?
- Career changes, job losses, seeking or leaving education (Financial Tower Moments)
- Loss of self - "I don't know who I am"
- Negative core beliefs such as: "I am worthless, hopeless"
- Unexplained feelings of grief, overwhelming sadness and sometimes, mental illness manifests, however this is thought of as a "spiritual depression"
- Repressed aspects of the personality rise to the surface (shadow, suppressed memories)

- Body aches and pains, digestive problems, sleep issues, fatigue, brain fog, affected appetite
- Begin to see the pain and injustices in the world, become repulsed and deeply affected by what is happening environmentally and in the news
- Wanting to go "home"

"Why me?"

Feelings of intense psychological suffering and emotional turmoil often manifest as anxiety and depression, which then takes over the physical body. It then is no longer able to make healthy and nutritious choices because deep down, they do not feel worthy. How you feed yourself is an indication of how you feel about yourself and that is incredibly difficult for our loved ones with eating disorders, which may get worse during a spiritual awakening. It is important to seek help from medical professionals and supplement this with naturopathic/holistic medicine until you feel well and clear enough to discern what your body needs.

"Why am I here, what is my purpose?"

Many of us feel insignificant, but do not realise the impact we have on the world. During this dark period, a soul can feel so lost, wandering in the dark, wishing and begging for relief. All the answers are inside of us, as is the light. It is terrifying to feel alone and it is truly a harrowing experience. However, something that helps is the sense of community, to resonate and collaborate with others. We must work to live, not live to work. Money is a man-made concept and more will always come. Having faith is arguably the most difficult aspect; when you feel doubtful, ask the universe for a sign!

During my spiritual awakening, there were a few different things that spoke to me and brought me comfort. The majority are 18+.

TV shows such as:

The Midnight Gospel – The premise is about Clancy visiting other realities and planets through an avatar to experience the environment as the natives do. It's very funny and has some interesting perspectives. It is a co-creation from Adventure Time's Pendleton Ward and Duncan Trussell. The animation is really fun to watch and I laughed out loud watching this and sobbed profusely.

Bojack Horseman – This is another cartoon and may be triggering, particularly for those with childhood trauma may find this difficult but, it is a fabulous watch and very relatable. The animation is great too. The humour is dark and the characters have a story arc that is both sobering and relatable.

Music

Music can also be extremely cathartic. The 70's era was one of free love and psychedelics, incredible musicians such as Jimi Hendrix, huge gigs like Woodstock, rejection of mainstream and capitalist agendas. The documentaries, music videos and books make for interesting viewing and reading about a whirlwind decade. However, music from any point in time can resonate with any person, and I find that really beautiful. Artists will never know how many lives they've touched, or how far their music has reached both physically and into one's soul.

Lyrics tend to speak to us:

"I had to fall, to lose it all, but in the end, it doesn't even matter" - Linkin Park

I feel this is a nod to stoicism personally, because once you get through these difficult times, you realise you don't actually need any of that shit. Chester Bennington took his life after a long struggle with his mental health. Chester was a survivor of sexual abuse and tried to transmute his pain into art. I think he was successful in this endeavour.

Songs such as: "Another Brick in the Wall" – Pink Floyd, "Free Bird" – Lynyrd Skynrd and "Hotel California" by the Eagles, all had a commentary on addiction, dark underbelly of society or wrote about their perception of freedom. These three songs are also fairly long, over the usual three minute mark seen commonly across commercial music for radio play. It's quite common for bands like these to rebel in mysterious ways as some didn't want to be a cog in the capitalist wheel.

Speaking of which, Tash Sultana a self taught musician from Victoria, Australia, writes and performs in their home studio, touring and encouraging fans to put their spin on the album. Tash is an incredibly talented musician who suffered from drug induced psychosis when in highschool after consuming a pizza with magic mushrooms on the top. The music written and created during this tumultuous time slingshotted Tash into stardom, but they refuse to conform to the "pop star notion." Their net worth is around 1 million dollars in comparison to other artists who work with brands or influencers. This is not necessarily a bad thing, but I do appreciate someone using their platform to share themselves and not for monetary gain to excess.

There are incredible artists and musicians who use their platform to incite change in society. The 80s in particular had a variety of artists who refused to conform, such as Prince, Boy George, Grace Jones, Pete Burns – androgynous people who had open gender fluidity and wrote lyrics about spirituality and sexuality which paved the way for current artists.

The classic by Salt N' Pepa, "Push It", inspired women globally to start talking about sex baby, and female pleasure. "WAP" is all about consensual sex and female pleasure which is why it gets people riled up, a lot of people do not want women to accept their sexual nature. When an AFAB person is sexually aroused, the area will be lubricated and they will be active, consensual participants in the sex. This is very rarely approached in music, and is groundbreaking in terms of mass education of female pleasure.

Madonna for example, even her name is a biblical reference – referring to the virgin Mary and baby Jesus, is proud of her sexuality and feminine nature.

Then moving onto film, we already discussed The Matrix earlier, but two incredible movies that depict intense social situations and require someone who is divinely guided to step up are:

Apocalypto – a film directed by Mel Gibson (who, coincidentally was made out to be a mad man for telling everyone that Hollywood was full of paedophiles… the truth always seems crazy at first). This story focuses on a chief's son of a tribe, thought to be somewhere in the Amazon. He experiences the dark night of the soul but is the one chosen to break out and lead his wife and child to safety. The gods and astrology favour him as he claws his way to a new way of life.

Interstellar – an incredible insight into realities and timelines alongside incredible performances from

Matthew McConaughey that tore my heart into pieces. Leaving behind the ones you love to save the collective is heart-wrenching. It is also incredibly accurate in terms of what we will be experiencing in terms of climate change. We have just witnessed Jeff Bezos' launching into space instead of him revamping his business model to be environmentally friendly or sharing his immense wealth with his employees and fellow humans.

What the protagonists of these films experience are "Tower moments." Katniss Everdeen must overcome a battle royale to protect her sister from a sinister government in "The Hunger Games." She goes through intense psychological suffering before emerging victorious although wounded from her suffering, which takes her decades to heal from as stated in the final book, spoiler alert.

Tower moments

The night of the dark soul? Or a time for transformation, only you can discern which it is.

If you've seen the Tower card in a Tarot reading and mouthed "oh shit", then you are not alone. However, the Tower has incredible possibilities and opportunities and when you tap into your intuition, start believing in yourself: you will know when these tower moments are coming. You can prepare as we prepare for each new season by looking out our winter boots, for the inevitable rain and cold.

Like many other beginners, I used to be afraid when I saw the Tower. Now, I realise I am the star of my own movie, and I am getting a preview from the cards of what's next. How you put a positive spin on things does not have to make sense to anyone else bar you!

For anything new to come in, the old has to go. This is why we must practice detachment because when we hold on to things they become stagnant and die. Like the moon, we have our phases, and all good things come to an end. In order to accept this, we have to allow our emotions to come to the surface and express ourselves. Once the emotional energy has been released we can observe the scenario from a higher view and acknowledge the Universe has our back. We humans generally get in our own way 99% of the time. A Tower moment doesn't have to be a major, dramatic event. It is an occurrence that is life-changing, and sometimes you don't realise until you reflect, which is why it is vital to reflect often. A Tower moment brings upheaval and changes, but again if you follow your intuition, be kind to others and generally live a good life - you'll be able to see these coming and take the lessons as blessings.

This is a great chance to build upon a solid foundation, although it may be painful or uncomfortable - it is always a blessing.

Saturn Return

The Dark Night of The Soul, Tower moments and the Saturn Return are all intrinsically linked. They all represent aligning with your true purpose, which usually requests you to shed your skin. At this point in time we tend to lose much of what we gained, working towards our thirties.

Saturn is the second largest planet in our solar system and sixth from the sun. Its rings are made from rock and ice and are surrounded by many moons; the most commonly known moon is its giant, Titan. It takes 29.4 "Earth" years to orbit the sun. Saturn is a large planet and has large responsibilities to match. This planet rules over life lessons; it controls authority and discipline. Many people have feelings towards Saturn, due to its diligence of responsibilities. It highlights our need for boundaries and limits, depending on what house it appears in the natal chart and transits in the return, you can identify what the themes are.

In astrology, the rising sign, also known as the "ascendant", is the sign that is displayed as the main personality. Many people assume they fall into their sun sign in regards to traits, which they do – but, one purpose of the rising sign is to make it to the Saturn Return.

Many people throw away old thought patterns and toxic environments as they near their thirties. Many of us go through a spiritual awakening around the same time! We peel back layers as we age and go through a Saturn return again around the age of 50. Saturn transits generally take between 2-2.5 years, with the return moving through all 12 signs, spanning nearly 3 decades. We can predict where the Saturn return will fall by using a profection wheel.

Astro Seek Profection Wheel - https://horoscopes.astro-seek.com/annual-profections-astrology-calculator

You will need to identify Saturn in your natal chart at the time of your birth. You can then check where you are astrologically using age, which will inform you of the house, sign and planetary ruler of that year. This needs to be looked at alongside the Saturn return, because it all intersects. There are many moving parts to astrology, but the great news is, there is tonnes of incredible information and teachers out there. Like maths, much of astrology is constant and factual, based on evidence and predictions. Old school forecasting! This builds the picture of the Saturn return. I always look at the profection year before and ahead to get a full idea of what is going on.

This is a cosmic rite of passage that can begin as early as age 26/27, depending on the rest of the chart. It helps shed the skin of our childhood and young adulthood, shaping us into who we need to be for this next chapter in our lives.

Saturn checks if you've done your homework. This planet tests you and will correct you when wrong. It can be a really difficult time for people as they feel everything they do is wrong. This is the Universe shifting things for them through Saturn, so that problem areas can be troubleshot and solved.

It sounds really tough, and it can be. However, if you have been putting the work in, a Saturn return can be a prosperous and abundant time. For example, my return is in the 6th house, where I need to focus on healthy routines and work/life balance. My return is in Aquarius which means I need to break free of conformities and find what works for me. Fortunately, I started to work on these areas prior to my Saturn return and am now reaping the benefits.

I personally believe we are in the Age of Aquarius, whether we are in the pre-shadow phase as it shifts from Capricorn, or truly in the swing – it's clear that Aquarian ways are here. The Age of Aquarius brings exponential growth in technological processes. We have seen that come to fruition with the rise of bitcoin and electric cars such as Tesla. It also speaks of unity, compassion and humanity coming together as one, and balancing the masculine with the feminine, who will be oppressed no more. We had the Age of Pisces; the fish is associated with Christianity and Jesus Christ, and was the age of divine masculine.

Unfortunately, this became twisted into a patriarchal society which brought mass destruction and is precisely the opposite teachings of Christianity. Our technological advances can help save our planet, so we must use this knowledge in a positive way. If this book has found itself in your presence, this is your call. It is divine timing. Heal yourself and you heal others. Take care of our Earth and try to make positive and ethical choices, financially permitting. These acts build up to a huge movement and I can express how much you are needed. Wake up. Stand in your power and see how vast the universe is.

The hero's journey

Why is spirituality considered cooky or wacky? Many people are still afraid to say that they practice alternative religions or manipulate energy through practices such as tai chi or witchcraft in its many forms. A spiritual awakening usually comes with a loss of friends, so you might as well accept yourself and not try to hide your esoteric practices. People will always judge, so why not do what you want to do? As long as you are not harming others, dress as you please, listen to the music you enjoy, and you'll find people who share similar interests.

If you feel unwell or unsafe please do seek help. For people of sound mind, you may feel as though you are losing it. I was ready to volunteer as a psychiatric inpatient during the worst part of my dark night of the soul. I was convinced I had lost my mind. As I began to work through my shadow work intensely I realised the art of detachment played a part in why I kept parts of myself hidden away. Why was I so embarrassed? Who cared if people thought I was mad? In the words of Lewis Carrol, "we're all mad here." No one is getting out of this alive, so why wouldn't you embody that main character energy? If people think you're a scary witch let them. Be you, be kind and you'll attract like-minded people who you can share and learn from.

True happiness starts to appear when you stop giving a shit about what others think, that is their business. This doesn't mean to ignore others when they challenge or trigger you, but never allow someone to disrupt your peace on your authenticity; you are an agent of free will as are they. Spirituality is about learning and growth. Returning to the community and giving what you can without draining yourself dry. Spirituality is about boundaries, managing yourself and your reactions so that you can help other people. No one can pour from an empty cup.

You may notice the book talks about protection quite a lot and this is due to the low vibrations of others affecting us. No matter how you practice to ensure that you believe in yourself, no one can take that power away, except you. Self belief is a powerful magic: it's a free tool, an infinite resource that can be tapped into. A boat can sink if the water gets in;

the water metaphorically speaking is other people's views, negative energy, social programming, doubt and a lack of mindset. "Your perception of me, is a reflection of you."

What's even funnier, is that we are all in some stage of "the hero's journey", a cycle that raises our consciousness and includes the dark night of the soul. After going through the dark night, and a Saturn return, most people find a lot of peace in their thirties and forties and happily integrate what they've learned from these difficult experiences.

It is also during these times that people align themselves with either religion or esoteric practices such as tarot or astrology. These are techniques to help you access the source-energy.

Chapter Three - Astrology

The twelve zodiac signs are as follows, in order: Aries, Taurus, Gemini, Cancer, Leo, Virgo, Libra, Scorpio, Sagittarius, Capricorn, Aquarius and Pisces. This runs from March to March, where Pisces meets Aries.

There are many sceptics when it comes to Astrology, as it is deemed a pseudoscience. A common theme here is people acting badly in the name of Christianity, similar to modern-day suicide bombers – who consider themselves holier than thou, these people are not true Muslims. We cannot tar people with the same brush who twist religion for their evil agenda. Anything of the occult became forbidden, cast out and became a reason to murder women. Hanging, drowning and burning of wise women became a daily occurrence, and so much knowledge was lost. These women were doulas, midwives, healers, doctors, nurses and teachers, the backbone of society.

Astrology is confusing to many and requires a degree of intuition, which struck fear into men's hearts. It has continued to be studied, and now we are able to create a picture of what is affecting us astrologically because it is so much more than your sun sign.

To create this astrological image, you must find out your birth time and place for the most accurate results. The big three are: the sun sign, the moon sign and the rising sign, also known as the ascendant. There are lots of free resources online, AstroSeek in particular is a great site to use as it creates a chart that can be saved with lots of different options for charts and in detail horoscopes. This site is not affiliated with us in any shape or form, this is just the site I use personally to create charts.

Personality

Sun sign

This is commonly known as your zodiac sign and is the one people mainly identify with. Most people know their sun sign and it can easily be checked in this chapter as we discuss the signs in detail. The sun sign is the embodiment of your highest good and asks you to step into your gifts, goals and true self. This describes your daily personality and identity.

Moon sign

This refers to the emotional side, how we manage our habits, what our deepest desires are, essentially everything hidden under the surface. It describes our vulnerabilities, insecurities and weaknesses.

The moon and sun sign combined give a clearer idea of a personality.

Rising sign (ascendant)

This affects the social personality, physical body and outward appearance. This is the energy that sets the bar for you astrologically. Many astrologers see the rising sign as a mask or a shield, which we use to protect our true natures until we are settled and able to be authentic. The rising sign is also the first impression we give off to others.

The rising sign is very fickle, unlike sun signs which get a whole month to themselves. Rising signs are all down to the exact minutes of your birth.

Houses

1st House

First impressions, firsts all round! This house is ruled by Aries, meaning if you had Aries rising, in the 1st house, Aries season would be particularly strong for you (the term is "exalted"). All the best aspects of the 1st house in Aries would shine through, magnified.

2nd House

Income, money, self-esteem. It also refers to material items and immediate environment. This house is ruled by Taurus.

3rd House

Communication, ruled by the best communicator of them all, Gemini. This also rules technological gadgets, siblings and neighbourhood community.

4th House

The house of family foundations, particularly how you were mothered, how you nurture yourself. Family dynamics and parents fall into this house which is ruled by Cancer.

5th House

Ruled by Leo, this house is all about romance, playfulness, drama and creativity.

6th House

Health and stable routines, is right up Virgo's street. It also describes being of service to others.

7th House

Relationships across the board, ruled by Libra.

8th House

Ruled by Scorpio, the house of mystery, other people's finances, sex, birth and death, transformation! Having this in placement in Pluto, would be exalted.

9th House

Morals and ethics in this house are ruled by Sagittarius. It also rules over luck, gambling, optimism and higher learning.

10th House

Ruled by Capricorn, it gets severe up in here. Government, boundaries, fathers, public image, career and success are ambitious Capricorn to the max.

11th House

Aquarius rules networking, friendships, community, all things technology and futuristic.

12th House

Pisces in the 12th house, where everything has an ending. Surrender.

Opposite houses and polarity

1st and 7th – Aries and Libra: SELF and OTHER

2nd and 8th – Taurus and Scorpio: STRUCTURE and TRANSFORMATION

3rd and 9th – Gemini and Sagittarius: RATIONAL THINKING and SPIRITUAL THINKING

4th and 10th – Cancer and Capricorn: NURTURING HOME and AMBITIOUS CAREER

5th and 11th – Leo and Aquarius: PERSONAL and COMMUNITY

6th and 12th – Virgo and Pisces: MUNDANE vs MAGICKAL

The goal here is to balance and compromise both houses. If you have lots of planets in a sign, in the same house (also known as a stellium), look to the opposite house and sign for information on how to balance this.

Empty Houses

An empty house means there are no natal planets in the house. People worry that this means they are lacking in this particular area, but this is not true. There are 10 planets and 12 houses, they will not all be full. These empty houses could be areas in a past life that have already been completed.

House & Description

1st

Come across easy going

2nd

Easiness when handling finances or securing stability

3rd

Easy communication, sometimes expression

4th

Harmonious home life

5th

Easily connects with the heart and creativity

6th

Integrates structure, routine

7th

Ease with relationships and commitment

8th

Easily inspire and transform others

9th

Expansion and pursuing opportunities

10th

Goals and responsibilities are easily managed

11th

Friendships are started and maintained

12th

Comfortable with death and transformations, how you let go of things

Inner planets are transit planets that move through the zodiac signs, applying their energies to the rules of that house.

When first learning about the planets, it helps to use these affirmations to understand how they affect you.

I AM

The Sun's masculine energy is exalted in the summer sign of Leo. This enormous star details our ego and power. The sun shines through our identity and describes our creative ventures.

I FEEL

The moon governs cancer, and describes the feminine energy. The moon sign tells us about emotions and how they are ever changing.

I THINK

Mercury is exalted in Gemini and Virgo, the fabulous communicators of the zodiac. It manages how we think, communicate and learn.

I LOVE
Venus, in the sultry signs of Taurus and Libra talks about romance and sensuality. It also describes the things we enjoy and see beauty.

I ACT
Action and getting things done. Mars is exalted in Aries, the fiery passion drives our ambitions. Mars in the natal chart describes where we expend our energy. Mars in a fire sign for example would be assertive, whereas Mars in Cancer would be far more passive.

I GROW
Jupiter dances in Sagittarius, it's natural placement. This planet is all about luck, prosperity and growing as a person. It also describes luck and success, in the natal chart, so look and see where Jupiter is for you. Jupiter expands.

I ACHIEVE
Saturn is at home in Capricorn, ambitious, steadfast and diligent. Saturn constricts and can teach us some difficult lessons. It makes us aware of our limits, boundaries and impulses. Natal Saturn can show us where we feel blocked energetically.

I EVOLVE
Uranus in Aquarius is future thinking, transformative but can also be rebellious. Learning to use your Uranus natal placements can detail how to better

use intuition and make predictions that will benefit you.

I DREAM

Neptune, god of the sea rules over Pisces. Neptune is in charge of psychic abilities and spirituality. Neptune moves very slowly, and is often referred to as a "generational" planet, as its cycle round the Sun takes 165 Earth years.

I EMPOWER

Pluto in Scorpio notes the happenings underneath the surface. Again, this is a slow moving planet and can be considered generational too, 247.9 Earth years spent on one rotation of the sun by this dwarf planet. This can show us where our transformations need to happen and if we are accepting of these changes.

Retrogrades (rx)

From Earth, it looks as though celestial bodies move in reverse; the planetary energies are turned inward and we are often asked to reflect. A retrograde can affect us before and after the planetary retrograde, often called "retro-shade."

Mercury rx - This planet is all about communication. How do you speak to people, communicate, are you responding or reacting? Check emails and important work for typos and mistakes. Avoid signing any major contracts during this time unless it was already in motion prior to the retrograde. This is also the time for ex partners or friends to make an appearance, the dreaded "what are you up to?" at 1AM. If you use this retrograde to your advantage, you will laugh and go back to sleep!

Saturn rx - A time of karmic balancing, meaning if you have been trying hard to be a good person, do kind things and still have a backbone - this will be a pleasant time. It gives us the opportunity to straighten ourselves out and get back on track. It is also time to create a routine to manage your health and social relationships. We should be having a lot of leisure and creative time alongside work.

Jupiter rx - The lucky giant calls us to go inward, and the rewards are great if we put the work in, we can achieve something previously deemed impossible.

Venus rx - This can be a difficult time and can bring about some drastic change in the areas of love, relationships, finances and creative sectors (Taurus and Libra's houses 2/8). This doesn't mean breakup's galore, relationships that are meant to last will come out of this period better off.

Retrogrades in the natal birth chart are believed by some karmic astrologers to be clues of past lives. It can also describe different tastes or ways of thinking that differ from those in your immediate family/circle.

Fixed stars

Fixed stars gain power through inter-planetary connections (conjunct/parallel) and the house it transits. It requires a deep knowledge of latitude and longitude, information I have yet to master! I will discuss three stars below as an introduction. Working out fixed stars in the natal chart can be confusing, there are many aspects to consider and I recommend working with paper copies that you can annotate.

I have chosen three stars that interest me, and are not hugely known. The research was tough to come by but I found it incredibly insightful when I studied the fixed stars in my chart.

There are lots of fabulous resources online, such as: *https://www.constellationsofwords.com/the-fixed-stars-in-natal-astrology*

Algol (B Persei) - also known as the "demon star" is about 93 lightyears from Earth.

Saturn and Mars like in nature, meaning it takes on traits from both planets depending on what else is happening on the chart. For example, it can be fatalistic or note legendary status. Artists such as Salvador Dali have this fixed star in their chart, as do Princess Diana and John Lennon. Renowned horror writer Stephen King, also has natal Algol.

Algol's night-time eclipses previously baffled astronomers, but the star follows a pattern; 3+3+13=19 and 19+19+19=57 days cycles. The Ancient Egyptians didn't know that the star was also eclipsed during the day, in some cycles. Algol is eclipsed by a close star that orbits Algol, thus blocking the view from Earth.

This star tells a story of violence.It is the source of the myth of the gorgons, since Algol falls within the perseus constellation.

Medusa's head was decapitated by Perseus, it can be seen when the constellation is drawn that Perseus holds Medusa's head, and in this point lies Algol.

The common story talks about the slaying of the gorgon, but there is an alternative story to be heard. Medusa was a victim of rape by Poseidon and asked for help from her dear friend Athena, who granted her the power to turn men to stone with one glance. Rape has been comitted for millenia, it is not about what you are wearing, it is about power. This power dynamic changed the course of Medusa's life; she was villianised for using her new found power to assert and defend herself. It notes intense female passion and power, and it requires confrontation and integration of Algon's lessons.

This can also mean,"losing one's head" in stressful situations where they are not in control.

Equally, the light side of Algol is a person facing everything head on, and winning. Their perseverance and endurance are the exact traits of a warrior. They do not let the fear stop them, and reach their goals and successes regardless of the challenges. This aspect depends on the natal chart and conjunctions with other planets.

Sirius is an Alpha star in the Canis Major constellation and is found at the mouth of the dog. It is Jupiter and Mars-like in nature.

The entire constellation is often mistaken as Sirius, which is a single star and not the collective. Sirius is the brightest star in the sky and gives planets such as Venus and Jupiter a run for their money in terms of sparklingness. In Ancient Egypt, it was held in such high regard because it signalled the rising tide of the Nile river, and people knew to head for higher ground. It was a message gratefully received.

Sirius describes a person who often walks alone. They tend not to fit in and eventually stop trying to. When Sirius is beneficial in the chart, it details legendary status, fame and honours, it also describes dangerous scenarios with dogs. *(I have Sirius natally in my 11th House and have been bitten three times so far, by a stranger's dog).*

Acrux, also known as "The Southern Cross" is the smallest constellation in the sky, but is also one of the brightest. This constellation can be seen in the Southern Hemisphere and can be found on country flags such as Papua New Guinea. It takes on the nature of Jupiter.

It notes burdens, trials and responsibilities, martyrdom and struggles. Equally, it can also represent the piscean nature of the mysteries of our universe, and being gifted psychically.

If fixed stars are of interest, I recommend seeking out a professional to go through your natal chart and pull the information for you.

Astrological events

There are also important astrological events that have taken place.

Y2K

Those born before the year 2000, have witnessed the turn of the century from MMI to MMM, a rare event indeed. Many people were fearful on New Year's Eve of 1999 that Y2K would shred the servers, the world would go dark and planes would fall out of the sky.

December 2020 conjunction

Last seen in 1623, the planetary kiss of Jupiter and Saturn occurred on the Winter Solstice in 2020. There will be another two, a conjunction in 2040, then again, thankfully in a more visible point in the sky - 2080.

Halley's Comet last visited Earth in 1986, and will not be seen again until 2061, appearing once every 70 years, essentially a once in a lifetime event.

The Degree Theory

Nikola Stojanovic wrote the book "The Degree Theory" and it is equal parts genius and intuitive. Degree theory can be used to discern further information astrologically. In each slice of the zodiac wheel. There is a zodiac sign and a house number which are unique to the person. Each slice represents 30 ° degrees, and within this a degree, say 5° for example, one would read the passage for 5 ° in Leo. If the zodiac sign is different from the degree theory sign, also read 5 ° for the sign that you have.

To explain this a little better, here is an example:

A client has Venus in Cancer in the 8th House at 23°.

23° is an Aquarian degree and I would read the passage for this. The client doesn't have the full Aquarian experience with this degree, as it is in Cancer. Thus, leading me to read the passage of 23° in Cancer to grasp the full picture.

23° Cancer reads "A charming person who may use his gifts for a good cause. A good critical writer, he can blend truth with his imagination to make his works interesting. They have the audacity to be different. "

23° Aquarius says "Denotes a remarkable mentality in men. (Not so favorable for women.) Usually kind hearted and charitable, but subject to trial and tribulation."

I would then look at Venus in the 8th House, discern the meaning from that and start to create a document of how the client experiences and gives love.

I have to use the rest of the chart to draw more information before making my conclusions, but that is a little insight as to how I work.

There are different ways to apply degree theory, this method works for me but may not resonate with others.

https://www.astrologyinserbia.com/e/nikola/tajna_svakogstepena.htm

"Important disclaimer: symbolic degrees belong to a branch of fatalistic astrology. Their interpretation must be regarded with the utmost caution, especially given the fact that different authors give different meanings to symbolic degrees. This is of course the reason why they are not included in our Astrotheme reports. However, they might interest those who are fond of this very ancient and fatalistic form of astrology."

Nikola also writes: **"**so, I began with the following analogy: If the 8th degree corresponds to the 8th sign of Scorpio, then the 1st degree has to be analogous to the first sign of Aries; the 2nd degree is analogous to the second sign of Taurus; the 3rd degree is analogous to the third sign of Gemini, and so on up to the 12th degree which has the symbol of the 12th sign of Pisces"

There is also the "decans" degree theory where each sign is divided into three sections. I find this method helpful when reading about my sun sign, but also use Nikola's theory and Sabian symbol interpretations. I tend to read degrees as follows: 3 degrees Taurus Sun, so I would check the Sabian description for Taurus, and the third degree is that of Gemini, so I would check that too and then apply what resonates, and be aware of both descriptions.

https://docshare04.docshare.tips/files/23078/230782881.pdf

House cusps

When someone is born around the time of one sign ending and the next beginning. This does not change your sign, rather it means you can display traits of both signs.

Aries-Taurus, aka the Cusp of Power: April 16–22

Taurus-Gemini, aka the Cusp of Energy: May 17–23

Gemini-Cancer, aka the Cusp of Magic: June 17–23

Cancer-Leo, aka the Cusp of Oscillation: July 19–25

Leo-Virgo, aka the Cusp of Exposure: August 19–25

Virgo-Libra, aka the Cusp of Beauty: September 19–25

Libra-Scorpio, aka the Cusp of Drama: October 19–25

Scorpio-Sagittarius, aka the Cusp of Revolution: November 18–24

Sagittarius-Capricorn, aka the Cusp of Prophecy: December 18–24

Capricorn-Aquarius, aka the Cusp of Mystery: January 16–23

Aquarius-Pisces, aka the Cusp of Sensitivity: February 15–21

Pisces-Aries, aka the Cusp of Rebirth: March 17–23

Source: https://www.mindbodygreen.com/articles/zodiac-cusp-theory-debunked

Shared houses

Each house is 1/12th of the circle. The zodiac signs go round the outside of the wheel and are not necessarily in line with the set houses of the chart. For example, Taurus and Gemini may share the 3rd house in an individual's chart.

Different chart styles:

- Natal – charts include Tropical, Vedic, Sidereal, Draconic
- Horary – used for divination, asking a specific question at a specific time to get an answer, creating a birth chart for this question
- Electional – great for events such as proposals or weddings using the planets and transits at the current time
- Mundane – prediction of events relating to society and government, it requires some form of pattern recognition skills
- Medical – As seen in the chart above

- Relationship Synastry – blending of charts between two partners to assess romance compatibility

House rulers and planetary rulers

This can get confusing. My personal recommendation is to compile information on the planet, the house, and the sign. Some planets in a certain sign or house will be difficult, such as Mars, a fiery planet being in watery Cancer.

Trines, sextiles and other aspects

Here comes the maths! Don't panic, this isn't too bad, and the great thing is there's no pressure and it's ok to need help. Checking and referring to notes is a great way to reward yourself with confirmation that you are correct. Eventually, it will become ingrained and you will rarely have to check.

Beneficial Aspects (also known as benefic) are usually blue lines in astro charts, such as Trines.

Trine

When you hear the word trine - 'think three'. A trine is a triangle with three points in the natal birth chart representing a harmonious aspect between celestial bodies 120° apart. This details your life path, once you get on it, things tend to flow. A grand trine is when each point of the triangle hits a different element. For example, a landed on earth, b on fire and c on air would make a Grand Trine. Some say this is a reward, from a past life due to it being such an auspicious aspect! Happy days.

Transit Trines occur and offer insight into how to best utilise the cosmos!

Sextile

Work it! Good things can come through effort and diligence. These angles are 60° apart and describe polarity, opposites. An example would be Aries and Gemini. April Elliot Kent (Practical Astrology) said: "My teacher once described the Sextile as being like a cross between a Trine and a Square; it yields the gifts of a trine if you're willing to do the work of a Square".

Maleficent Aspects (malefic)

Oppositions (polar opposites) integrated this becomes a gift! 180° degrees apart creates a hard aspect known as an Opposition. There can be a push-pull quality here, which can be further intensified with planetary polarity. Opposites attract, so what benefits can you take from the sign? A Taurus can be stoic, so perhaps taking an active step in being more emotional like Scorpio, would be beneficial.

Conjunctions (0°) can be benefic or malefic depending on the planets sharing the house and the sign of the house where the conjunction falls. It is also dependent on planetary relationships. Conjunction astrologically describes how close planets are to each other and how their energies blend together. A stellium can be found in natal birth charts, where three or more planets are conjunct. (I have a Capricorn stellium, of 3 planets and a north node and must balance with the opposite house and sign).

Astrology Chart

Aries is a Fire sign, which is ruled by mars and represents the first house.

Taurus is an Earth sign, which is ruled by Venus and represents the second house.

Gemini is an Air sign, which is ruled by Mercury and represents the third house.

Cancer is a Water sign, which is ruled by the Moon and represents the fourth house.

Leo is a Fire sign, which is ruled by the Sun and represents the fifth house.

Virgo is an Earth sign, which is ruled by Mercury and represents the sixth house.

Libra is an Air sign, which is ruled by Venus and represents the seventh house.

Scorpio is a Water sign, which is ruled by Pluto and represents the eighth house.

Sagittarius is a Fire sign, which is ruled by Jupiter and represents the ninth house.

Capricorn is an Earth sign, which is ruled by Saturn and represents the tenth house.

Aquarius is an Air sign, which is ruled by Uranus and represents the eleventh house.

Pisces is a Water sign, which is ruled by Neptune and represents the twelfth house.

Earth signs

Taurus, Virgo and Capricorn are the earth signs of the zodiac. This element is known for its nurturing side, as in anything you give an earth sign will be grown in their garden. They have patience unparalleled and the perseverance to see things through. In matters of the heart, Water signs are a good match.

In Tarot, they are represented by "pentacles or coins" and are the financial powerhouses of the zodiac. "Materialisation" is the word associated with earth signs. Like everything in this universe, there are light and shadow sides to the zodiac signs. Earth signs are practical, hard-working and value stability. They like material things but it is not always "flashy", more so "if you buy cheap you buy twice." However, this trait can be expressed in some.

The Dark Sign for Earth is CHAOS. Use the chaos! Embrace passions, strong instincts and deep desires. Earth signs tend not to believe in themselves so this is essential to their growth. Earth signs should dance, sometimes they plough along their path and forget to let loose.

Dark signs are taken from The Alchemist: https://www.magicalrecipesonline.com/2019/04/your-shadow-element-based-on-your-zodiac-sign.html

Taurus

20th of April - 20th May.

Ruler – Venus

Opposite sign – Scorpio

Tarot – The Hierophant

Now, this is probably the most in depth I have written across the zodiac signs, because I am a taurus sun. I am writing from my direct experience as the bull.

Patient, diligent, enjoys comfort: you will likely find them wrapped up in a blanket or wearing comfortable materials. They enjoy eating and sleeping and have a notorious reputation for being lazy. However, when integrated properly, this is a form of self-care. Some Taureans need to do something for themselves before starting a task, to pour into themselves and access energy. A Taurus may have a nap before finishing an important deadline, and they will feel better about it.

These signs should avoid getting stuck in a rut. They are incredibly loyal and steadfast, but sometimes to their own detriment. They must shake off habits that do not serve their highest good. They need a clear purpose to help them identify the path to take and remind themselves of what they are working towards. Taureans have a strong understanding of their emotions and should continue to work on their self-awareness. Taureans are ruled by Venus and are sensual beings, they require a partner who is going to take the time to make them feel good. They are a glutton for sensations, any sensory input is a thumbs up!

Health

Taurus rules the throat chakra – so throat, neck and vocal cords. This sign can cause stress. Their main health risks are: ENT issues (sinuses), Thyroid (hyper/hypo/autoimmune), Diabetes Type 2 from poor diet management and can suffer from depression. For a Taurus, "everything in moderation" is a great mantra. Taureans should sing to tap into additional life energy (as well as a nap!).

Virgo

August 23 – September 22nd

Ruler - Mercury

Opposite sign - Pisces

Tarot card – The Hermit

Like Gemini, they are ruled by mercury which makes them apt communicators. They are very logical and analytical, able to sort and compartmentalise. However, if you hurt a Virgo, don't expect to hear from them again – they cut things off that don't serve them. They have very high standards and continue with the perfectionist streak that earth signs are well known for. They are meticulous and are known for their impeccable memory. They can be critical and have a hard time turning off, they must set a boundary with their work/life balance.

Health

Although Virgos can be calm and collected, they can suffer from nervous stomachs, riddled by anxiety as large events come up on the horizon. This sign is meant to trust their gut, their butterflies, because this is how their intuition manifests. They also need to watch out for issues with the spleen and constipation.

Capricorn

December 21st – January 20th

Ruler – Saturn

Opposite sign – Cancer

Tarot card – The Devil

Capricorns are so ambitious and these placements climb and climb and climb. Their success tends to come in their mid-years and depending on their other placements, can become wealthy due to their perseverance and ambition. They are realistic and practical, always realistic. This placement tends to overcome hardships.

Health

Capricorns struggle immensely with stress but do begin to manage this better as they age. They must work in moderation so as not to make themselves ill.

They are naturally affected by skeletal issues and have problems with their knee joints.

Air signs

In the words of Fleetwood Mac – "you can go your own way", is exactly what air signs do. They go where the wind blows them, but since everything else circles the sun, they can rebel and go off to be free spirit. Air signs are very influential, born to stand out, and they need to be reminded not to conform or people please. They are true liberation and at the forefront of changes in their surroundings, workplace and even country. Air signs are fabulous communicators and are represented by the Suit of Swords in Tarot. The Dark Sign for Air is OBLIVION, where they should practice the art of detachment.

Gemini

May 21st - June 20th

Ruler – Mercury

Opposite sign - Sagittarius

Tarot card – The Lovers

Two-faced or duality? Gemini's get a bad rep, Libra also has another side to them! Geminis are multifaceted and have many talents. They are natural conversationalists and put people at ease. The duality in their nature is not "two faced" but rather appropriate personalities for the appropriate occasions. They can be fun, spirited and carefree but can also turn serious for a more solemn conversation.

Health

Due to their impeccable communication skills, Gemini signs and placements can experience social burn-out, insomnia and are prone to vascular, skin and joint disease. As always, a healthy diet and exercise (perhaps something fiery like salsa?) to get the blood pumping.

Libra

September 23rd - October 22nd

Ruler - Venus

Opposite sign - Aries

Tarot card - Justice

Depicted by the scales, Libras are known for balance. They can struggle with being alone, feeling as though they need someone on the other side of the see-saw. Known as "mirrors", Taurus and Libra placements reflect others. Libras enjoy balance, symmetry and equality, but can be conflict-avoidant in order to keep the peace. Libras are good communicators and seek out intelligent stimuli, whether that is music, art, books, film, tv, outdoor activities such as mountain biking. I know two Libras who love to cycle in nature.

Health

Kidneys, skin, lower back (sacroiliac joint) are points of contention for Libras. Stay hydrated, avoid crash diets (Atkins) as they can cause kidney stones, as can overindulgence in alcohol. The skin is the largest organ of the human body and requires far more respect than it is given.

Aquarius

20th January - 18th February

Ruler – Uranus

Opposite sign - Leo

Tarot card - The Star

Aquarians like their fellow air signs require mental stimulation but also more alone time than Gemini and Libra. They are very progressive thinkers and can see perspectives from both sides. Aquarius is ruled by Uranus, who transforms us. They can change and metamorphose with ease whilst the rest of us are lagging. Sometimes Aquarian signs can come across as cold due to their deep intellect, so they must work on sharing emotions and vulnerabilities. They are able to see themselves in predictions of the future, then go after that image.

Health

Aquarians should watch their ankles and circulatory system. The lymphatic system is powered by our movement, particularly by our legs. When we walk, we actively push our lymphatic fluid around the body which allows toxins and waste products to be removed. Movement is vital. Wear good ankle support and rest strains and sprains using the RICE method (rest, ice, compression, elevation).

Water signs

Ah, the deep, deep signs of the zodiac – Pisces, Cancer and Scorpio. Known for their emotional depths, empathy and compassion. They are particularly in tune with the balance of life and death and are ruled by Pluto. In Ancient Greek Mythology, Hades of the Underworld was responsible for happenings under the surface. The Disney film Hercules really does him no justice. Like the dark side of the moon, he represents the shadows, secrets, intuition and integration of the psyche. Secrets are not always inherently bad, and what is done in the dark will always be revealed in the light. Water signs are painted as overly sensitive and emotional, and must balance themselves with fire energy – they need a purpose, they must embrace their emotions too otherwise both of these things will leave them swimming in circles, exhausted. Water signs and Earth signs are compatible in terms of love. The Dark Sign for Water is VOID, where emotions should be felt but not always acted upon.

Pisces

February 19th to March 20th

Ruler - Neptune

Opposite sign – Virgo

Tarot card - The Moon

Pisces natives are deeply empathetic and like their siblings, it is also a sign of sensitivity. They are great at building emotional relationships and are incredibly tolerant. They have strong feelings that can be hidden under the calm surface, which is sometimes to their detriment. They will become closed off if they are continuously taken advantage of, and therefore must implement the boundary setting traits of Virgo.

Health

They are emotionally sensitive and this is reflected in their lymphatic system, which can retain fluid when overwhelmed or stressed. The lymphatic system is powered by movement, particularly by the legs, so using a foam roller, GuaSha, walking, yoga or swimming will help. Like a body of water, they are sensitive to toxic substances and must be careful about what they consume.

Cancer

June 21st – July 22nd

Ruler - The Moon

Opposite sign – Capricorn

Tarot card – The Chariot

This water sign has a tougher exterior than a Pisces but is equally emotional on the inside. They can ride a wave and saunter about the beach and are very adaptable to different environments. This is true for Cancer signs and they also rely on intuition to help guide them. Although crabs are not biologically "home bodies", the zodiac signs are. They love to nest and cosy up with a loved one, which is why Earth signs tend to match well with Water signs. Cancer and Taurus sun signs get on particularly well. Sensitive Cancers represent the 4th house and its maternal aspects. This sign is ruled by the feminine energy of the Moon, making Cancers emotional people. Learning to balance such emotion can be difficult, which is why having a creative outlet is paramount for the crab.

Health

They have a delicate stomach which can be disturbed by emotional upset. Water signs don't tolerate alcohol well, it poisons the water so to speak, and should avoid it. Cancer signs are susceptible to weight gain in later years, which is not a negative thing - but are you gaining weight healthily or is there an underlying medical issue? There are many reasons why someone is fat but it is nothing to be ashamed of, fat bodies are beautiful.

Scorpio

October 23rd - November 21st

Ruler - Pluto

Opposite sign – Taurus

Tarot card – Death (can also be associated with The Tower, due to the nature of Pluto)

Dark and mysterious, ruled by Pluto the celestial god of transformation, death and rebirth. Scorpios are social beings and can make great leaders, due to their emotional nature, protective shell and a stinger for... well. They love and hate fiercely, more so than other signs. They can be jealous lovers, although dedicated. They need to transmute emotions positively and identify what their emotions are trying to tell them. Play detective.

Health

UTIs and yeast infections can plague Scorpio big three placements. It is vital they hydrate well, avoid alcohol, urinate after sex and reduce their sugar intake, as yeast infections feed directly on sugar (the fermentation process for bread and beer require high amounts of sugar), needless to say, the body is not trying to sell baked goods.

Fire signs

Sheer energy. This fire energy is all about the sun. They are passionate, fiery beings and although they can burn you, the scorched earth becomes rich in nutrition and growth – or another common metaphor is a phoenix dying and rising from the ashes. These signs are good with the destruction of the old and bringing in the new, as this is exactly what fire does. The energy fire signs need to tap into, is the dark sign of "darkness.£ This asks the fire signs to embrace themselves when their spark is extinguished, as death and rebirth is fire's bread and butter. These signs are represented by the deck of wands in tarot. The Dark Sign for Fire is DARKNESS, and asks you to embrace your humanity, everyone is both light and dark.

Aries

March 21st - April 19th

Ruler - Mars

Opposite sign - Aquarius
Tarot card - The Emperor

Competitive and passionate beings, fueled by fire. Another sign that appreciates honesty, sometimes they can be blunt. They are incredibly driven and tend to lead the way, the only way out is through! They struggle to pace themselves and adapt, which can cause friction in their intimate relationships, if everything is done their way or the highway.

Health

Aries tend to ignore doctors advice, most likely because they don't want to slow down or be held back. Aries rules the noggin so, head issues such as migraines, neurosis, teeth and also blood disorders, due to anger mismanagement they can be susceptible to alcoholism.

Leo

July 23rd - August 22nd

Ruler - The Sun

Opposite sign - Aquarius

Tarot card – Strength

The Lion is proud, and they are selective about who they welcome into their pride. They are actually very hardworking, it's just that socialising comes to them so naturally. They are very passionate people and also romantic partners. They struggle with listening to their internal voice, with the constant roaring. They must listen to themselves and others, to become wise to experience.

Health

The heart, spine and back are areas a Leo must keep an eye on. They are proud people and will do anything for those in their pride, even to the detriment of their health. They must find the line between helping and self-sacrificing.

Sagittarius

November 22nd – December 2st

Ruler - Jupiter

Opposite sign - Gemini

Tarot card - Temperance

Boundless enthusiasm and energy, a Sagittarius will always get the party started. They are travel bugs and often feel the urge to get away and explore; a Sagittarius likes to have some sort of getaway planned. Curious people, but they can be tactless at times with their words. Like other fire signs, they often struggle with patience.

Health

Hip problems and liver issues are common complaints for Sagittarius placements. They must use their fire to exercise and keep things moving to avoid stagnation. Weight tends to stick to the hips.

Heavy drinkers will see this reflected in their skin, which will become coarse.

Chapter Four - Tarot Cards

The History of Tarot

Tarot Cards do not necessarily have occult-ish beginnings, as it was once a parlour game for people to enjoy. It seems as though the Italians played this game, reciting poetry inspired by the imagery. Since creativity and intuition are usually linked, a book was eventually written detailing the imagery and supported esoteric descriptions and how to divine them.

Their origin may have started in Africa, primarily Ancient Egypt, but there are also links to Asia. It isn't easy to know for sure, so the cards are steeped in mystery!

What is the purpose of Tarot?

Well, what are you looking for?

I ask questions out loud to the cards, asking for clarification. For example, "what do I need to know today?" is a simple way to begin reading. There are spreads you can use as a beginner, working up to more intricate spreads. There is no wrong way to divine. I have added in sticky notes to help me channel messages or remember what something represents in this particular query.

What can it do? What can't it do?

The cards can highlight some future aspects, pick up on past energy, and reveal the present, but most people don't realise there are always choices and free will. It helps give me insight into something I am confused or unsure about. I always seek information, so having a source and a connection to the Universe is a joy. Ask questions and listen. Some people might experience clairaudience or have visions. Tarot is a tool to open yourself up to the whispers of the Universe.

Major Arcana

The Major Arcana consists of 22 cards in total, and only 21 are numbered, which starts after "The Fool." When Trump cards appear in a reading, you are asked to take the overall energy into account. Think of them as the main themes of a reading. Each card has a light and shadow side, as does the Minor Arcana, which is reflected in the upright and reversals.

0 - The Fool

"It's time to trust my instincts, close my eyes and leap" – Elphaba, Defying Gravity from Wicked.

The Fool is not foolish: they are immersed in the world around them and trust the Universe to catch them when asked to fall. They follow their heart, and the path is being lit for them; it may look as though they are walking blindly when this person is divinely guided. They only look like a fool to others who do not understand. 0 is the number of potentials; we can make something from nothing.

Upright – Enthusiasm, blind faith, taking a leap of faith, naivety, innocence, new beginnings,

Reversal – Lack of discipline, not in control, substance abuse, risk-taking, negligence

1 – The Magician

The Magician has the power to create their reality. They can manifest their hearts desires and manipulate energy (not always a negative thing!). They have incredible potential that can be tapped into, but they must believe in themselves.

Upright – Psychic abilities, great potential, resourcefulness, logic, willpower

Reversal – Blind or ignorant to talents, manipulation for greed, trickery

2 – The High Priestess

This is a wise woman, a fountain of knowledge, inner knowing and self-sufficiency. This archetype is often personified by Persephone or Isis, queens of the underworld.

Upright – Intuitive, psychic abilities, listen to your inner self for guidance, science, evidence, a guide/mentor

Reversal – Mistaken, ignorance, blocked third eye

3 – The Empress

This card often depicts the divine feminine; she is the embodiment of nature, Aphrodite and Venus exalted. In readings, she brings the theme of abundance and fertility.

Upright – Beauty, nature, abundance, fertility, joy, sensuality, nurturing of self and others, harmonious relations

Reversal – Smothering others, lack of growth, insecurity, disharmony

4 – The Emperor

The divine masculine counterpart of the Empress. He describes stability, stepping into your power and reaching your highest potential. He has an equal partner to support him in his endeavours and offers the same to the Empress. This is the blueprint for equality in relationships, remove the gender roles and treat each other as humans instead.

Upright – Stability, father figures, authority, ambition and success

Reversal – Controlling or abuse of power, issues with paternal figures, overbearing dominance

5 – The Hierophant

Another wise being, preceded by their excellent knowledge and advice, the Hierophant indicates a spiritual teacher. This card asks you to consider the ethical, spiritual and different viewpoints of others.

Upright – Sharing knowledge, beliefs, discussing religion/spirituality (this is incredibly personal, so apply own values first)

Reversal – People taking your kindness for weakness, not taking the good advice, non-conformity, rebellion

6 – The Lovers

The duality of a person can be depicted in this card. It also represents the love, trust, unity and effort of a relationship.

Upright – A balanced and harmonious relationship or a choice to be made (follow your intuition)

Reversal – Shadow work is required to help make the necessary choice and manifest better things

7- The Chariot

Full steam ahead! This card says you are on the path to victory.

Upright – Fame and fortune, others seeing you as a source of inspiration, ambition, ploughing ahead on your purpose, KEEP GOING!

Reversal – Lack of direction, coercion, revenge, war, a person putting energy into hatefulness

8 – Strength

Often the Strength card has a kind woman wrangling a lion or sometimes holding its head. Not every approach requires forcefulness, and a soft touch is a good option.

Upright – Overcoming obstacles with empathy and compassion, courage, endurance, success

Reversal – Vulnerability, self-doubt, weakness, lack of confidence, abuse of strength

9- The Hermit

It is time to reflect and go within. This could be a spiritual mentor or finding the path to awakening yourself.

Upright – Alone time is needed for healing, gaining insight and wisdom during this time of introversion, self-analysis and shadow work

Reversal – Betraying yourself by not expressing what you think, betrayed by friends or family, isolation. This reversal explicitly says to ask for help.

10 – The Wheel of Fortune

When this card appears, it is fated. There are set points in time, but many different paths and interactions led up to these events. When this card appears, it is destiny.

Upright – Luck, success, lottery wins, gambling wins, abundance

Reversal – Luck running out, not being on time, learning how to overcome obstacles

11 – Justice

This card describes logical and rational thinking to reach a conclusion. It can also describe karma, a lesson or a reward.

Upright – Getting what you deserve, contracts, commitments

Reversal – You are getting a lesson or 'punishment', adverse legal outcomes or proceedings, inadequate commitments

12 – The Hanged Man

Total surrender. In Norse mythology, Odin hung from a tree for nine days to receive wisdom and insight.

Upright – Spiritual development, gifted, divine, psychic ability, waiting but using it as a time to learn

Reversal – Illness, sacrifice, prison, suicide by hanging – if you practice fatalistic tarot/astrology

13 – Death

Transformation. "*And in the spring I shed my skin, and it blows away with the changing winds*" - Florence Welch perfectly describes the Death card.

Upright – Cleansing, releasing what doesn't serve you, transformation, ego death, letting go of toxic habits or addiction

Reversal – You are avoiding the necessary changes and prolonging the pain. Holding on to the dead things for too long will eventually poison you

14 – Temperance

The Temperance card describes a harmonious home, end of the conflict, management of finances.

Upright – Good management of home life, savings, contentment

Reversal – Conflict avoidant, mismanagement of resources, overlooking obvious problems

15 – The Devil

The Devil card describes our Earthly pleasures becoming too much of a focus; we tend to bind ourselves to people and things.

Upright – Addiction, substance abuse, poor mental health, caging oneself and avoiding shadow work, negative sexual connotations

Reversal – Overcoming all of the above

16 – The Tower

One person has dived out; they know why they've jumped and what they are facing, but the other person was pushed, representing resistance to change – regardless, it's happening!

Upright – Disaster in money, relationships, business – you will need to apply what resonates and use clarifying cards.

Reversal – I read this card as the person who leapt out the window. Accepting changes, integrating them, learning the lessons, rising like a phoenix

17 – The Star

The light at the dark end of the tunnel, very apt, considering it follows The Dark Night of The Soul – The Tower Card. This shining star brings hope and healing.

Upright – Wish fulfilment, reassurance rewards are on their way, hopeful feelings for the future (a sign you are on the way out of The Dark Night)

Reversal – Jealousy from other people, doubt, believe in yourself and the Universe, use your energy positively

18 – The Moon

An incredibly complex card to decipher at times, so use clarification. The Moon depicts a variety of things from emotions, secrets, hidden agendas to psychic abilities.

Upright – Femininity, things not as they are but not bad, intuition, psychic gifts, fear and anxiety, worrying, deception/illusion,

Reversal – Releasing fear, overcoming illusions and getting to the bottom of things, regaining composure, negative energies, all is not what it seems for the worst

19

– The Sun

Here comes the sun! With the light of day, incomes new energies and a new chance. It is a relatively positive card.

Upright – Achievements, success, abundance, positive energy, trips abroad, happiness within family, marriage, soulmates

Reversal – Blinded and not seeing the truth, overlooking the negatives and only seeing the good

20 – Judgement

"Turn and face the strain, Ch Ch Changes!" - David Bowie

Revelations, changes, awakenings, entering the next cycle, whether it's a slow burner or you are bursting on the scene.

Upright – Fresh starts, a wakeup-call you do not ignore, change of status

Reversal – Ignoring the calling, not meant to be, something outwith your control

21 – The World

Completion of a cycle, sit back and celebrate your success. Consider this a graduation!

Upright – Desired outcomes, ending of a cycle, positive results, travelling

Reversal – Delays, but it's all still happening

Numerology

Numerology is the study of numbers within spirituality. It is strongly correlated with Angel Numbers. In the words of Cady Heron in the movie Mean Girls: "numbers are the same in every language." The universal approach to numbers can be deciphered below:

Meaning

1

You may be struggling with negative thoughts or a lack mindset, the number 1 represents beginnings and asks you to face the changes.

11:11 is a typical number to see when people first start to become spiritually awake.

2

Balance is on the way; if you are in a tough spot, it will change. Keep the faith. This could be a sign regarding a relationship.

3

Love, wisdom and dreams are coming true. Sounds good! Associated with good luck and fortune. Keep learning.

4

Manifesting requires a leap of faith. The Universe will always provide for you and this requires personal growth.

5

Show gratitude! Listen to your five senses and be guided by your intuition.

6

Show yourself some love. It may be a trying time surrounded by fear and anxiety. Positive affirmations and journaling can help.

7

A lucky number. This sometimes notes a spiritual awakening. It is also connected to new opportunities.

8

On its side, the number eight looks like the infinity symbol. It is a sign of prosperity and abundance.

9

You are bringing light in. Keep sharing your truth and wisdom with others. Make sure you also pour into yourself.

10

Completion in Tarot card readings.

Upright and Reversals

Some Tarot users do not read reversals; it is entirely up to you how you'd like to interpret the cards. I find them helpful, especially as you become more intuitive and knowledgeable about the cards. I believe the Tarot requires study and practice; many will find it tough to pick up a deck and start divining from scratch.

Minor Arcana

Suit of Wands

Fire sign energy – Aries, Leo, Sagittarius

This refers to: energy levels, transformation, passion, ambition, career drive, sex, making moves, travel, phallic/masculine energy.

Wands in terms of timing can signify days, as in the message should arrive within the week. However this can be difficult to intuit and generally experienced psychics can pick up information about time, but it does usually fall to divine timing and that can really be whenever!

Ace of Wands - New beginnings, new sexual encounter, creativity, an excellent time to start business endeavours

Image – A hand holding a powerful wand emotes a positive feeling

Reversal – Seeking sexual gratification and thrill-seeking in whatever respect

Two of Wands - Future planning, discovery, progress

Image – The crossing over of wands means collaboration, indicates partnership, possibly business. Implemented changes will be successful.

Reversal – Getting what you wanted but realising you are not happy

Three of Wands - Success, accomplishment, inner peace, desires satisfied.

Image – Three wands all crossing over again, which could represent the trinity for those who are religious.

Reversal – Group work, the introvert's nightmare, awaiting clarity

Four of Wands - New job, relationship, positive news to celebrate, so show some gratitude!

Image – Balanced wands, interspaced.

Reversal - Attachment, lack mindset, needing to belong

Five of Wands – Friendly competition, sports, an opportunity to grow, an exciting challenge

Image – Balanced wands, interspaced.

Reversal – Jealousy, feeling unworthy,

Six of Wands – Recognition and accomplishments, a reward whether this is emotional or financial, depends on other cards

Image – Balanced wands, interspaced.

Reversal – Being arrogant or appearing arrogant to others, success going to your head, ego issues

Seven of Wands – Coming out on top of a power struggle, standing your ground, maintaining principles, negotiation

Image – Balanced wands, interspaced.

Reversal – Haters, people trying to ruin you or conflict within interpersonal relationships

Eight of Wands – Everything coming together, really positive card! Messages, communication, social media, welcome news

Image – Multiple wands crossed over, describing balance and abundance.

Reversal – Moving too fast, struggling to manage, juggling work/home/love/social, gossip, social media being a burden

Nine of Wands – This card especially requires clarification because it can have a few negative connotations upright and reversed. Delays, sickness, breaking off/up, injuries. It can also confirm suspicions and waiting for the right time

Image – Balanced wands, interspaced.

Reversal – Feeling as though nothing is going your way, feeling let down and disappointed, plans cancelled, misfortune or even disaster.

Ten of Wands – A good ending requires hard work and effort. Pushing yourself, increased energy, effort and sacrifice working out for success

Image – Balanced wands, interspaced.

Reversal – No end in sight, insomnia episodes, work is too much

Page/Knave of Wands

Personal growth, uncomfortable almost in that growth period. Immaturity becoming maturity through drive and ambition. They look upwards and out in an optimistic manner. They are surrounded by fire, which is a reminder not to get lost in the fire; stay true to yourself. This could be the birth of a new idea, relationship etc.

Upright – You could be integrating your inner child with creativity and playfulness. This card also describes imminent communication. In a spread where you are querying others, the court cards of wands represent fire signs (Aries, Leo, Sagittarius)

Reversal – Delays and setbacks, uninspired or procrastinating, possibly dealing with an immature person.

Knight of Wands

The Knight is depicted on horseback in the traditional deck, with a wand in hand, ready to charge into battle! He is a hero on horseback. The Knight has stamina, confidence and sexiness. Remember, this energy is not gendered, so you must apply it to the people in your life.

Upright – New home, moving (in many contexts), risk-taking, the action being taken, work being done, passion, imminent, wanting to complete things and succeed

Reversal – Arrogance, recklessness, impatience, passive, no self-control

Queen of Wands

A passionate Queen, they support you by ruling as your equal. They have an air of the occult around them; a black cat usually sits at the feet of the throne. This person is independent and self-sufficient.

Upright – Passionate, self-confident, sexy, charismatic, optimistic person. They have uplifting energy and will support you.

Reversal – A fiery temper, jealousy, not meeting your needs whilst demanding their own

King of Wands

Pure creativity, light and power surround the King and the staff. This person is a natural-born leader and good at implementing creative ideas. They look forward to all sorts of challenges and rise to the occasion.

Upright – Sticking to a goal, being passionate and driven, creates their own reality.

Reversal – Rash decisions, arrogant, selfishness, aggressiveness, hasty decisions

Suit of Cups

This suit describes emotions and relationships. It also notes Water sign energy – Pisces, Cancer and Scorpio. In timing, it can mean months.

Ace of Cups – Filled with deep joy, expressing feelings that can't be contained (find an outlet), new opportunities, great love (romantic or platonic).

Image – An overflowing cup

Reversal – A missed opportunity, blocked creativity or emotional loss.

Two of Cups – Appears during love readings, often referred to as “the second Lovers” card. Meeting a kindred spirit or soul family member, Details a beautiful and intense relationship.

Image – A cup of love each

Reversal – Trust issues, imbalance in the relationship, tension in the friendship

Three of Cups – Happiness, gratitude, infectious feelings that influence close ones around you. People are genuinely happy for you, and it's time to celebrate.

Image – Cups “cheers” overflowing

Reversal – Partying too hard, indulgence, distance (either in location or in relationships), gossip

Four of Cups – Hitting a plateau, boredom, disconnection

Image – Two cups on either side

Reversal – The reversal is positive and notes someone choosing to be positive, be aware and accepting—Practise detachment.

Five of Cups – Mourning, loss, grief, disappointment

Image – Some decks have an eye crying into a cup

Reversal – Again, positive in the reversed position. Acceptance and peace, moving on.

Six of Cups – Restoration, healing, memories, ancestry work (spiritual or genealogical)

Image – Balance of three cups on either side

Reversal – Leaving home, moving forward, independence.

Seven of Cups – Searching for a purpose, making choices, daydreaming in older interpretations could be described as manifestation

Image – Many cups

Reversal – Confusion, lack of purpose

Eight of Cups – Walking away and leaving something behind

Image – Many cups

Reversal – Avoidance, fear of change, fear of loss, lack mindset

Nine of Cups – Inner happiness, satisfaction, luxury, emotional stability

Image – Many cups

Reversal – Smugness, dissatisfaction, lack of true joy

Ten of Cups – Wish fulfilment, dreams come true

Image – Many cups

Reversal – Emotional immaturity, disappointment

Knave/Page of Cups

A burst of inspiration, the inner child, being creative, a sensitive idealist. This card wants you to follow your intuition, particularly anything inspired from within. This card asks you to make a creative outlet for yourself, whatever that may look like.

Upright – A happy surprise, a creative person, try and tackle the issue from a different angle, or ask for fresh eyes

Reversal – Creative block, emotionally unavailable person

Knight of Cups

This Knight has embraced his feminine energy and integrated the feminine and masculine aspects of the psyche. If it is a person, they follow their heart.

Upright – Artistic, graceful person, diplomacy, good negotiator, compassion

Reversal – Allowing emotions to rule your life, unable to take action, jumping to conclusions

Queen of Cups

A powerful intuit, similar to the High Priestess in the Major Arcana, the presence of this card describes a person who is aligned with their intuition or stepping into their psychic abilities. She asks us to fill our cup before helping others.

Upright – supportive nature, psychic, emotional depth, sharing resources

Reversal – Pouring from an empty cup into relationships or work, imbalance

King of Cups

A king who has emotions, compassion and the ability to discern using intuition and logic to make good decisions that benefit many.

Upright – The head and heart are in alignment with love, balance, wisdom,

Reversal – Manipulation of emotions, lack of control, staying in a job that drains you

Suit of Pentacles

The suit of Pentacles represents finances, material items, property, nature, stability and long term future plans. It also represents Earth signs: Taurus, Virgo and Capricorn.

Ace of Pentacles – New financial beginnings, savings, abundance, money manifestation

Image – A hand palm up, holding a coin

Reversal – Poor financial planning, lack mindset, excessive spending, scarcity, instability

Two of Pentacles – Finding balance in finances, love or some aspect of your life

Image – Often looks like the pentacles are placed in a figure of eight, the infinity sign

Reversal – Poor balance, poor financial decisions or choices in general

Three of Pentacles – An apprentice learning and studying, hard work, effort, commitment to quality work

Image – Often depicted as coins in a trine or engraved into a building

Reversal – Not learning from past mistakes, unwillingness to learn and poor quality of work

Four of Pentacles – Holding on to: past issues, past people, hoarding, stinginess, security

Image – A person sitting in wealth, holding a coin, one on their crown and two under their feet

Reversal – Finally letting go, generosity, sharing

Five of Pentacles – Temporary financial hardship, feeling left out, homelessness, divorce, breakups

Image – Pentacles make up a stained glass window

Reversal – Improvement in the areas mentioned in the upright position

Six of Pentacles – Gifts, generosity, community, charity, sharing wealth and kindness

Image – A person, is sharing the wealth with others in the Rider-Waite edition

Reversal – Money/gifts with strings attached, subservience or inequality, scams or a mean person

Seven of Pentacles – Hard work paying off, rewards and results, manifestations, perseverance, and can describe someone returning to your life

Image – Pentacles on a bush, money growing on trees

Reversal – Bad business or financial management, not finishing what you started, laziness and impatience

Eight of Pentacles – New job or self-employment, trade reputation, expertise, attention to detail and achieving goals

Image – Someone working on a project surrounded by pentacles

Reversal – Don't be a perfectionist and don't be affected by failures

Nine of Pentacles – Success, achievements, large purchases, security, living in abundance

Image – A person surrounded by two trees with many pentacles in each

Reversal – Boring job, failure, under qualified or a workaholic

Ten of Pentacles – Surprise windfall of money, inheritance or a lump sum, business, marrying into money

Image – Five pentacles top and bottom in balance

Reversal – A disputed inheritance or will, family feuds, financial disaster, false marriages or relationship as a means to a purpose

Page of Pentacles

The page brings news, turning ideas or communications into action.

Upright – Good news, solid beginnings on a good foundation, good prospects, loyalty, Earth magick

Reversal – Lazy, lack of goals, underachieving, magick used negatively or to manipulate

Knight of Pentacles

A hard worker, a consistent effort through tried and tested methods will ensure success. Sometimes it will get boggy; keep your head high and moving through

Upright – Slow perseverance, patient, stubborn, working with nature, making dreams and wishes come true

Reversal – Impatient, apathetic, no common sense, gambler, materialistic

Queen of Pentacles

The love of this woman should be accepted gratefully, for she is truly a gift.

Upright – Mature person or grounded and stable, business-minded, generous, witch/healer, organised, successful, very wealthy

Reversal – Scared to dream big, too attached to materialism

King of Pentacles

Upright – Hard work paid off, success, resting at the top, maintaining

Reversal – losing grip of control, slob, greedy, bankruptcy

Suit of Swords

Ace of Swords – Everything beginning to take shape, a great love, medical treatment

Image – A hand holding a sword upright with a good grip

Reversal – Great hatred, things moving too quickly and unable to choose, cuts/accidents or painful medical treatments

Two of Swords – Use a different perspective, take a strong decision on something, make the choice, indecisiveness is impeding you, two offers, choices, roads to take

Image – A person blindfolded wielding two swords upright

Reversal – Being overwhelmed by fear and anxiety, being overloaded with too much information, lies being exposed

Three of Swords – A card of heartache, grief, loss, a period of difficulty or hardship emotionally, depression, trauma, take time to heal

Image – Three swords piercing a heart

Reversal – Overcoming the above, a card of optimism

Four of Swords – Feeling mentally overloaded, things you are experiencing are being made worse by fear and anxiety, you must go within and find peace

Image – Someone laid to rest with swords hanging on the walls

Reversal – Awakening, spiritual breakthrough, reintegration to the world with new views, take care of yourself you may be on the way to mental overload

Five of Swords – Surrender, walking away, can sometimes mean defeat, deception or lack of communication warns about violent crimes

Image – People picking up the swords post-battle

Reversal – Peaceful resolution, ending of conflict, compromise or sometimes an escalation of revenge

Six of Swords – Calmer waters and healing awaits

Image – A person on a small boat wrapped in a blanket, whilst another rows the boat. All the swords are standing upright on the boat

Reversal – Falling out of the frying pan and into the fire, slow healing, feelings of being trapped, standing your ground

Seven of Swords – Deception, lies, trickery, tactics, manipulation, being strategic, underhand behaviour

Image – Someone picking up five swords and running away, leaving two behind

Reversal - Confessions, coming clean, ignoring warnings, pathological liar

Eight of Swords – Backed into a corner, terror, psychological issues

Image – A person tied up, blindfolded, standing in a field of swords like a prisoner

Reversal – Escape, freedom, release, surrender

Nine of Swords – High fear and anxiety levels

Image – A person crying in bed with all the swords on the wall behind them

Reversal – Light at the end of the tunnel, recovering, improving, shame, regret, guilt

Ten of Swords – Not a great omen, backstabbing, gossip, severing ties

Image – A person dead, lying with all the swords in their back

Reversal – Rising above pettiness and gossip, near-death experiences

Page of Swords

This person can talk their way out of conflict; they know who they are and stand up for themselves. When this card shows up, rely on your intuition and gut feelings.

Upright - Protected, guarded, vigilant, delayed news, planning, thinking before speaking

Reversal – Gossiping with ill intent, spying on someone and then relaying information back, watching and judging everyone else

Knight of Swords

The Knight brings changes! It is time to seize the day and go with the flow.

Upright – if this is a person they are a great communicator, leadership qualities, intelligence, assertiveness

Reversal – Missed opportunities, out of control, rude, forceful, leading others to danger

Queen of Swords

This depicts someone stepping into your life and helping you solve a problem. This person may be very quick and intelligent.

Upright – Honesty, truthfulness, chatty, communicative, problem solving, constructive criticism

Reversal – Overly critical, pessimistic, poor communication

King of Swords

The King represents self-care and self-discipline; they are logical and reason. This person may be a deep thinker.

Upright -Structure, routine, power, authority, conversation, manners

Reversal – Lack of the above and can also be oppressive, judgemental, rude, weak

Tarot decks

There are a wide variety of Tarot decks to choose from, the original being the Rider-Waite. Choose a deck that you feel drawn to. It's very Harry Potter; "the wand chooses the wizard!" - you will also feel the energy and be drawn to things once you open up to the fact everything and everyone on Earth has a vibrational frequency.

There are Angel Oracle cards, self-care cards, twin-flame/divine counterpart cards; if you can imagine it, there is a deck! There is no need to purchase more decks if you are satisfied with the Tarot. I use extra decks to clarify and help me build a larger picture for readings. I would encourage people to visit their local occultist and support small businesses. Shopping in-store for Tarot decks will make it far easier to locate items that vibe with you.

A personal favourite of mine is the “Postcards from Spirit” deck by Colette Baron-Reid. They help me feel surrounded by my loved ones who have moved onto the next phase without being frightened, mainly because I have been visited by spirit before and found it frightening as a teenager. Sometimes you need some kind words and support.

The more aligned with your cards you are, the better the readings and intuition. Keep your cards dust-free! I maintain my cards by keeping them in their boxes when not in use, but I also protect them using crystals and stones, placing them either in the box or on top.

To bond with your decks, I recommend sleeping with the box by your bed or under the pillow. Alternatively, you can hold or shuffle the cards and talk to them, sing to them, introduce yourself to them and ask them to collaborate. This may sound absolutely ludicrous, but, as I said – everything on Earth has a frequency, and everything is capable of responding – just not in human ways. Dogs can hear at a far higher frequency than we could dream of, yet we accept this fact. This is another fact we must accept in order to evolve.

I would only "cleanse" my decks if I was giving public readings with the person in the room to remove their energies and mine for the next client. Spiritual hygiene is hugely important. Otherwise, they don't need cleansing. I don't allow friends or family to touch my cards; buying a second deck for readings is the best advice I can give.

How do Tarot cards and readings support empaths?

Doing Tarot readings for yourself helps bring yourself into alignment with the intuition that may be blocked or hidden away. You receive validation from the universe when you follow your intuition correctly, especially when you listen.

Tarot Spreads and Readings

PAST, PRESENT, FUTURE

Shuffle your cards and pull three cards, one after the other and lay them 1, 2 and 3. 1 being the past, 2 in the present, and 3 is the future. Divine! Seek clarification for each card by reshuffling the deck and asking what it is the original card wants you to know.

DAILY 1 CARD PULL

What will your day look like? This helps build intuition and a good morning routine. Later on, journal and discuss if you were in alignment with the card or not, and if not, why not?

There are some fantastic tarot tips from @TarotReaderPeter, who uses Instagram and Twitter. I recommend following occultists who you can learn from in an easy way – I really like how Peter explains things on their platforms.

Clarifying the cards

Asking the cards for clarification is very helpful when you are having trouble discerning what is going on. Shuffle and ask for clarification on a specific card that has already been pulled and apply the meanings. I wouldn't draw any more than three cards because it distracts from the rest of the spread. I would also encourage writing down your readings, conclusions, questions asked and solutions; this is what helped me grow the most.

Try:

- Talking to the cards out loud and asking for the support of the Universe or whoever you identify with for help
- Visualising the question or person in your mind's eye, you may need to close your eyes for this
- Looking at a photograph or a map whilst formulating the question if you need a physical, visual cue
- Writing everything down, questions and answers – make it clear and concise so that it is understandable when you refer back to it

https://www.thelawofattraction.com/meanings-numbers-0-9/

https://labyrinthos.co/blogs/tarot-card-meanings-list

https://www.collectorsweekly.com/articles/the-surprising-origins-of-tarot-most-misunderstood-cards/

Chapter Five - Stoicism

https://iep.utm.edu/stoicism/

Stoicism was a product of Ancient Greece and was consequently adopted by the Roman Empire. Socrates, Seneca and Marcus Aurelius are well-known stoics from this era. Athens was a hub for incredible thinkers. Zeno was a wealthy merchant who was shipwrecked in Athens, losing everything he owned. Zeno learned about the teachings of Socrates and thus created Stoicism.

To experience happiness, there are four virtues that one must follow—Courage, Wisdom, Temperance and Justice.

"The happiness of your life depends on the quality of your thoughts" – Marcus Aurelius.

"Whenever someone has done wrong by you, immediately consider what notion of good or evil they had in doing it. For when you see that, you'll feel compassion, instead of astonishment or rage. For you may yourself have the same notions of good and evil, or similar ones, in which case you'll make an allowance for what they've done. But if you no longer hold the same notions, you'll be more readily gracious for their error."— Marcus Aurelius.

As a side note, Marcus Aurelius was a Taurus, born on the 26th of April. I find many earth signs to be stoic in nature.

Stoicism is essentially the acceptance of life. Your mindset predominantly affects how you cope with experiences and events in life and can alter outcomes positively or negatively. The Universe will do its thing anyway, so having a positive mindset makes life so much easier! I am not referring to toxic positivity where we often hear "just be happy"; no, I refer to realist approaches. Cause and effect will change our environment, whipping around us like a storm sometimes, but the goal is to maintain a healthy mindset. Stoicism allows people to deal with the world as it is whilst seeking self-improvement and promoting growth in others to make positive changes in society.

Wisdom – Navigating difficult situations in an emotionally calm manner, seeking information and approaching things rationally. We cannot control anything but our response.

Temperance – Moderation and self-restraint, knowing that having enough brings abundance. How well do you manage the pleasures of life? And the burdens? Everything has to be balanced.

Justice – Equal treatment of human beings even when they have done wrong: "*seeking the very best in ourselves means actively caring for the welfare of other human beings."*

Courage – Facing each day with integrity, standing firm with your values and ethics. Persist and resist, they cannot move you. *"Nero can kill me, but he cannot harm me*" - Seneca.

A modern stoic and psychologist, Viktor Frankl, created "Logotherapy" from the original stoic concept "logos" which means "divine reason" after being held as a prisoner in a concentration camp. Through one of the darkest periods of his life, he realised that meaning must be created in life. He made new reasons to live when there were none, not in a traditional way, considering Frankl went through mass genocide. There is freedom in choosing to see life in your way, through the meanings you apply to it. You have to give yourself a reason to live and that can be as simple as being there to feed your cat daily because they would miss you.

Stoicism reminds me of "Ironic" by Alanis Morisette:

"A traffic jam when you're already late
A no-smoking sign on your cigarette break
It's like ten thousand spoons when all you need is a knife
It's meeting the man of my dreams
And then meeting his beautiful wife
And isn't it ironic, don't you think?

A little too ironic
And, yeah, I really do think"

This verse, in particular, brings people laughter because the old phrase "if you don't laugh, you'll cry" comes to mind. It is being able to hit every red light on the way to an important meeting and understand that it's happening for a reason instead of letting anger and fear of being late consume you.

Instead, calmly call ahead (hands-free, of course!) and inform them, driving calmly to your appointment. Otherwise, you'd become more infuriated and stressed by the time you got to the office. It is all about how you cope with things by adopting a specific mindset.

Lessons and blessings

Choosing to experience life as a series of lessons and blessings changes things considerably. Yes, bad things happen to good people and sometimes there is no closure or explanation. Endings can be devastating; new beginnings are terrifying. However, learning to embrace it all and choosing to integrate each unique experience actively brings wisdom.

I am not saying people shouldn't feel sad or angry, not at all. Rather, this ideology comes into play in the acceptance stage of grief, overcoming addictions and so on. This mindset needs to kick in at the depths of despair because that is how you start to break the social programming society instils in us.

Being caught at every red light is a divine sign to slow down. You are supposed to be taking a breather. Notice how calm and relaxed you are when each light is green? You pass through driving along contently because you are not rushing. All the green traffic lights are a bonus. You are calm and collected and it's a sign of being in alignment.

Chatting with a stranger in a public place can be a life-changing event. You never know when someone will cross your path and change it forever. By witnessing someone else's suffering and holding empathy for them, or discussing and debating points, making sure to listen to another person's experiences, all from a conversation could open you up to a different viewpoint.

Law of Attraction

Bob Proctor said: *"The law of attraction is always working, just as the law of gravity continues to work."*

The body holds energy at every moment, and this is moving and evolving whether we are aware of it or not. We require energy for a state change to happen in psychics, just as boiling water heated eventually turns to steam. Even as our bodies turn to dust there is vibration from the dust particles. Earlier in the book, we discussed physics briefly and noted that everything is made up of atoms. Atoms vibrate, we vibrate, everything is in a state of flux, and that is how we can change things in an instant.

Identifying the paradigm

A Paradigm is an amalgamation of – genetics, social programming, thinking processes and mindset vibration – ideas and thoughts control the body and what we attract. You attract people that are on the same frequency as you.

The conscious mind is the rational thinker as it is educated. It can create, accept and reject ideas. We learn through repetition, which then passes into the long-term memory and the subconscious mind. Unfortunately, this area is subject to propaganda and misinformation through media and TV and peer pressure.

The subconscious mind struggles to discern between what is real and fake; it is the opposite of the rational brain, irrational and emotional. It holds the profound aspects of the psyche, similar to what Dr Jung had described. It contains intuition, trauma, memories, addictions and other shadow aspects.

These two parts of the paradigm affect our physical body. If we are in a negative vibration, we will feel unwell. Likewise, we will feel well and seek out behaviours to support this if we align with a positive vibration internally.

Am I living the way I want to live?

What programming have you had to unlearn from childhood? Many empaths and highly sensitive people must undergo severe reprogramming through shadow work and therapy because they internalised so much. These people really absorb everything, and when you don't know how to protect yourself and care for yourself properly, you feel drained and lacking. Furthermore, when you go to school or a job you despise, it makes you more miserable each day. You actively begin to dread it, and suddenly everything else feels worse. You are in a lack mindset and, like gravity, are pulling negative vibrations towards you.

When breaking away from a particular mindset or shifting the paradigm, this tends to feel very uncomfortable. For example, Bob Proctor discovered that he needed "*Y type ideas to override his X programming.*"

For example, people who have received religious indoctrination go through stages of grief, beginning with denial and then anger. Then, as they receive more information and life experiences, they move through the pain and eventually reach acceptance. We must continuously meet new people, diverse people from different backgrounds and cultures to inspire growth in ourselves.

So how can you shift your paradigm, change your subconscious mindset, and align yourself to an abundant frequency?

Think about a result you're getting that you don't want, then ask yourself what behaviours or habits are causing that result. To change this, the following list from How to Change a Paradigm, can help.

- Write the behaviour out in precise detail
- Ask yourself what habit or behaviour is the polar opposite of the behaviour you just identified
- Write out the new behaviour on another sheet of paper
- Burn the paper that contains the bad habit (as a symbolic gesture)
- Write the positive habit out four or five times a day. Read it frequently. You will eventually lodge that idea in your subconscious mind

Manifesting

Now that you are aware of the law of attraction, you can put manifestation into practice. To help with manifestation, there are a few ways of doing things:

Create a vision board

Put pictures of your dream home, car, clothes, holiday destination, whatever it may be. If it is physical, stick it on your board; this gives you a clear goal in mind.

55 x 5 technique

Write down your manifestation 55 times in a row over five days. This can be changed to 111, 222, 333 and so on, whatever resonates or works for you.

Listening to abundance frequencies

Sleeping overnight with frequencies tuned to the same as money, for example, will attract better finances as the subconscious starts to accept the Y idea.

Orgasm

At the point of orgasm, visualise what it is you want. This is a powerful way to manifest, alone or with a partner. Lighting a green candle and setting the intention of financial abundance is another way to guide prosperous finances towards you.

Remember that you have to vibrate at the same frequency to "get" these things, so this is an excellent time to practice gratitude, patience and faith that it will all come to you because it will when you do these things.

Resonance

To resonate with something or someone usually means you are filled with emotions. For example, resonance in the body can feel like goosebumps appearing, which happens when you hear a particularly moving piece of music or scene in a film. So it is when a feeling or emotion is invoked within you.

Schumann Resonance

The Schumann Resonance measures the Earth's electromagnetic field. The resonance of the Earth is 7.83 Hz. Humans feel happy and healthy at this frequency. Humans are deeply affected by electromagnetic waves, but many refuse to identify this as an issue due to conspiracy theories etc. The Schumann Resonance is accessible to anyone; more information is available on the NASA website, and many intuitive or physics discern what is happening to the collective using this tool.

Many psychics use the Schumann Resonance as a point of reference to understand the energies we as a collective are experiencing on Earth. In early July 2021 we experienced solar flares which affected the Earth's magnetic field.

It's clear to see that soundwaves and lightwaves dramatically affect humans both positively and negatively.

Use of electromagnetic waves as a tool for destruction

As Hitler rose and rose to power, Hertz radio waves were hugely complicit in propaganda and brainwashing German citizens into genocidal compliance.

The Goliath Radio Transmitter was huge and could reach submarines globally at a depth of 20 metres. They also used radio waves to upgrade their flight and bombing systems, which was eventually blocked by a BBC tower that was used to jam the German frequencies. They also used the radio to lure German citizens in by putting on entertainment prior to Hitler's speeches.

Electromagnetic waves in science

Earlier in the book I mentioned that sensitive individuals are particularly affected by technology such as smartphones. This is due to the frequency of the smartphone and the fact it emits blue light, which impedes the brain's circadian rhythm. Our natural body clock is controlled by sunlight and the process synthesises a hormone called melatonin, which is blocked by the overuse of blue light and lack of blinking.

In a clinical trial 12hz frequencies were played to rhesus macaques (a type of monkey) to observe a memory improvement. Plasma levels showed increased melatonin (the circadian rhythm hormone) due to possible brain receptor activation.

Another study based on humans showed that EMF (electromagnetic fields) of 30 kHz to 300 GHz do have an effect. People who use mobile phones for over 30 minutes a day, with the phone to the ear, have an increased risk of a brain tumour called a glioma. Increased risk and cancer development can be managed by using a headset for work and eating antioxidant foods.

EMF products such as laptops and mobile phones radiate heat, making our ears and laps overheat. Therefore, minimal use or use with moderate breaks is essential for well-being. In a murine model, rats were exposed to 900MHz, prenatally, and were found to display hyperactivity, memory impairment, and the frequency had damaged their blood-brain barrier's permeability - https://www.ncbi.nlm.nih.gov/pmc/articles/PMC7642138/

A double-bling pilot study (2019) compared 440Hz and 432Hz on the human body. The results stated: "the data suggests that 432 Hz tuned music can decrease heart rate more than 440 Hz tuned music. The study results suggest repeating the experiment with a larger sample pool and introducing

randomised controlled trials covering more clinical parameters."
https://pubmed.ncbi.nlm.nih.gov/31031095/

Looking at WiFi exposure study in murine models:

"In the present study, WiFi exposure alters some neuro-behavioural function associated with neurological diseases. WiFi exposure affects motor coordination and alters exploratory motor function in exposed rats when compared to control. This is in agreement with previous studies where high radio-frequency electromagnetic radiation exposure induces cognitive impairment and stress-related behaviours in rats."

"This effect has been linked to the ability of radio waves to cross the blood-brain barrier (BBB) due to their selective permeability and ionisation properties. This is an indication that electromagnetic field exposure could result in neurodegeneration."
https://www.ncbi.nlm.nih.gov/pmc/articles/PMC5897318/#sec0105title

These are two studies found on Pub-Med. There are more, but user discretion has to be used here and apply critical thinking. Taking time away from screens is beneficial for your mental health and relationships.

Healing frequencies and binaural beats of the Electromagnetic spectrum

Moving on from the negative aspects to electromagnetic fields and frequencies, let us explore the positive aspects. Music can be healing and community experiences with music make some magical memories. We book wedding bands or go to gigs because we are united during that set, or that evening celebrating a couple.

The vocal singing scale, do, re, mi, fa, so, la , ti, do, is known as solfege which originates in the 11th century. Dr Joseph Puleo rediscovered the solfege and reworked them into healing frequencies. The solfeggio healing frequencies also have ties to Sanskrit chanting: OM, for example, is 432Hz, the frequency for aligning with nature.

Different frequencies and what they do

Dr Glen Rein, a biochemist, exposed genetically similar DNA vials to four kinds of music with different frequencies – Gregorian and Sanskrit chants and also rock and classical music. By measuring the rate of UV light absorption, an essential function of healthy DNA, the Gregorian and Sanskrit chants had the most healing effects by increasing DNA UV light absorption at approximately 5 to 9 %: https://www.relaxmelodies.com/blog/science-behind-solfeggio-frequencies/

Below are frequencies I recommend listening to along with their many benefits.

432 Hz OM

This is the frequency at the very root of the Universe. The benefits of listening to this frequency are: unity with nature relaxes the body and mind (more so than 440 Hz used by the Nazi regime). In addition, this frequency is very pleasant to listen to.

528 Hz

The frequency of love. It is a miraculous healing frequency and was used in practice to treat a BP oil spill in the Gulf of Mexico and was proven to reduce and remove toxins from the water, confirmed by analytical chemists. The Beatles were right; all you need is love! This frequency was proven to reduce anxiety in rats - https://pubmed.ncbi.nlm.nih.gov/30414050/

396 Hz

This frequency helps us achieve our goals. 396 is linked to our root chakra and helps ground us to maintain productivity. This frequency is excellent for transmuting grief and guilt into productivity. It helps remove any emotional blockages that may be holding you back, liberating stored energies from within the body.

639 Hz

This can be described as the communication frequency as it aids interpersonal relationships. This particular frequency can be used for creating harmonious environments for good communication to flow.

741 Hz

Problem-solving and cellular healing are the primary purposes of this frequency. It cleanses the body of electromagnetic radiation, detoxifies, purges the system and is also suitable for opening up the throat chakra.

852 Hz

This frequency is used to open yourself up to the Universe. In addition, this is used to balance the third eye chakra and promote psychic powers.

963Hz

Also known as pure miracle tones, music tuned to this frequency targets the pineal gland, which is said to be calcified in unawakened individuals. Thus, this frequency helps people wake up and break free of their programming to lead a more fulfilled life.

Use these frequencies to your advantage and listen to them especially when sleeping to experience the maximum effects. YouTube again has loads for free and they are also available on Spotify.

Binaural beats and brain waves

Binaural beats describe different frequencies played in the right and left ears. This virtual beat perception has the brain tune into neither of the frequencies but rather the frequency in-between the two being played. It sounds confusing, but this tuning helps the brain relax and can be used as a method for neuroplasticity because of the ability to affect neurons. Lower frequencies are better for relaxation and sleep, whereas higher frequencies are suited for arousal and activity. Examples of these frequencies are as follows:

Delta

1-4 Hz
This frequency is excellent for deep restorative sleep. A person is not in REM sleep, and this sleep stage is physically beneficial.

Theta

4-8Hz
Theta is more like the REM sleep stage: it is perfect for processing and committing long-term memory. It can also help access the unconscious, which can be incredibly healing for the psyche; however, if you

struggle with trauma or PTSD symptoms, please seek professional help.

Alpha

8-14Hz
This frequency brings on a relaxed, calm state. This is a good one to listen to when wanting to recharge and practise self-care when conscious. This is also a sign of mindfulness as there is not a focus on one particular thing.

Beta

14-30Hz
The Beta frequency supports concentrated mental activity, and you are awake, conscious and alert.

Gamma

30-100Hz
Gamma frequencies are excellent for intense problem-solving. You are in a workflow. Sometimes called the “genius brainwave”, it helps us reach a higher level of consciousness.

Epsilon

<0.5Hz
These brain waves are a sign of a deep meditative state rarely seen, but it is associated with spiritual insight and out of body experiences.

Using frequencies whilst sleeping is a great way to attract a partner or heal your body. These frequencies are directly tied to the Universe and are a fantastic way to manifest. Add an extra layer to this by writing down the manifestation and sleeping with it under the pillow as the frequency plays overnight.

Protection

Empaths and HSP are known to take on the energy of others, or at least, be affected by it. Internalising someone else's energy can show up as irritation, crying, aches and pains, headaches and so on. Have you ever suddenly found yourself crying for no reason? Only to stop even more abruptly than when it started?

It is therefore imperative to cleanse our energies and living space. In this chapter, you will find information on how to protect and heal yourself.

The frequencies mentioned earlier can be incredibly protective, sound is a wonderful way to cleanse and protect your space which is why many healing spaces have music on in the background, healers must protect themselves too when they open up to heal others.

The Evil Eye originates from Greece and Turkey, previously made from clay or ceramic, but eventually became a coloured glass. Called a "nazar" in Turkey, a teardrop-shaped glass amulet can be worn or hung in the house. It is a protective talisman to ward away any evil eyes that wish you ill will.

Some practitioners use sigils. A sigil is a word or a phrase stripped down into a symbol. You take away vowels and are left with consonants. You use numbers 1-9, with letters of the alphabet assigned a number to correspond to. Below that, a box with numbers 1-9 (looks like sudoku) is where you link up the numbers to create the glyph. It can be a little confusing. There are, however, apps for sigil making and online sigil generators.

Regardless of whether you make your own or print them out - charge them with the intention and the job you assign. Trinary: The Magick Web-App by Chaos Tarot has a generator you can use for free. There is also an option to tip them for their creation.

You can also visualise a tremendous white ball of energy. Feel it in your hands, create resistance and move the ball around. You can physically feel the ball of energy! Use this and visualise the white energy moving around the body. You can also imagine this as waves of light coming over you and clearing away what no longer serves you and as a barrier to protect you from any negativity outside of you.

Altars

Altars are a space for your gifts and spirituality to be honoured. You can make this space about deities, your ancestors or the change in the seasons. If you create an altar, make sure you give it a dust and tidy, set candles in a safe place and make it a sacred space

Altars are also about gratitude and this is an excellent opportunity to be thankful and remember what their ancestors went through. In African practises, they would pour some water or alcohol and set it aside as an offering for their dearly departed. The Day of the Dead in Mexican culture also has offerings in the form of food and drink and thoughts and prayers.

Crystals

Mining vs lab made

Many people are pursuing laboratory made crystals due to their ethical reasons and availability. They are fast becoming the choice for engagement and wedding rings. As they have not come from the Earth directly, some practitioners don't believe they have life. Whether synthetic or Earth grown, I believe it is all about intention and you can make your own mind up which you would prefer to use.

Below are some of the crystals attached to the zodiac signs:

Aries - Carnelian is used to ground these fiery beings
Taurus - Rose quartz enhances the venusian qualities that are innate to taureans
Gemini - Turquoise helps the throat chakra, which is essential for these communicators
Cancer - Moonstone for balancing emotions
Leo - Citrine, a beautiful bright crystal represents their life essence and vitality
Virgo - Virgos need amazonite for inner kindness
Libra - Pink tourmaline helps remove any patterns of inconsistency and self-doubt, which Libras are prone to
Scorpio - Ruby, a stone of creation which is needed to balance the plutonian vibes of death and transformation
Sagittarius - Sodalite will help unlock the third eye chakra, include this in your guided meditation practice for improved results
Capricorn - Peridot helps replenish the body and removes feelings such as resentment
Aquarius - Gem silica is a stone of peace
Pisces - Sugilite is excellent for spiritual development

https://hk.asiatatler.com/life/healing-crystals-zodiac-sign

Crystals and gemstones can be personalised for your use. Knowing your big three; sun, moon and rising sign means you can curate your own crystals specific to your needs.

Many crystals cannot be used in water and should not be cleaned this way. However, holding them in your hands and setting an intention or using incense, the crystal will be cleansed.Selenite is particularly helpful; it removes any negative energies and promoting healing in obsidian is a black stone that is powerful and protective. Tourmaline is also a good alternative.

Wearing a crystal around your neck or as a ring helps amplify the protective or healing powers.

Make sure you are purchasing ethically sourced crystals, or lab-made. We are now able to create laboratory crystals which takes the pressure off diamond mining considerably, more so for the people who are abused and manipulated to work for blood diamonds, which directly buy arms for militias. Please be careful about who and where you are purchasing from, please use buyer discretion.

History of crystal use

Ancient Sumerians and Ancient Egyptians were among the first societies to incorporate crystals into their jewelry for protective benefits. Many crystals have Ancient Greek origins as they attributed traits to particular crystals, as did the Chinese during the Han Dynasty where Jade was declared the royal gem.

Crystals and gem practice fell away with the rise of Christianity, as natural healing became more of a pseudoscience than a practice. However, as a collective we are once again moving forward with natural medicines combined with western medicine, which can only be a good thing in my opinion!

Chemistry and physics of a crystal

Amethyst, for example, is a type of quartz. It is composed of SiO2 (one silicon molecule to two oxygen molecules - silicon dioxide). These crystals are hexagonal and tend to have a mix of tall prismatic crystals with small thicker points. The surface of the crystal can also be striated. It can be found in different colours due to the varying levels of Hematite (Iron) or Magnesium, often seen in Amethyst from Thunder Bay, Nova Scotia in Canada.

We know that everything in the universe has a frequency and crystals are no different. "*Cymatics visually shows us how energy naturally expresses itself through harmonics, frequencies, and wavelengths while organically embodying geometry as it's building blueprint for matter*" - Hibiscus Moon. https://hibiscusmooncrystalacademy.com/lab-created-vs-natural-crystals/

Crystals and precious gems have strong, stable molecular structures. Their sacred geometry emits frequencies, just as everything does in this universe.

Crystal vibrations - Cymatics is the study of visible sound and vibration, a subset of modal phenomena.

"Ernst Florens Friedrich Chladni was a German physicist and musician. His most important work, for which he is sometimes labeled the father of acoustics, included research on vibrating plates and the calculation of the speed of sound for different gases. In 1787 he repeated the work of Robert Hooke and published "Entdeckungen über die Theorie des Klanges" ('Discoveries in the Theory of Sound). In this book, Chladni describes the patterns seen by placing sand on metal plates which are made to vibrate by stroking the edge of the plate with a bow" - (Delamora, 2021). https://www.delamora.life/cymatics

Through music and sand, the vibrating plates showed incredible geometric patterns that had been produced by different frequencies. Selenite, an incredibly healing crystal, vibrates at 244.5 MHz. The body has different areas vibrating but should usually be between 55 and 90MHz. This crystal is incredibly high vibrating with amazing qualities such as: healing pain/inflammation and can be used as a wand to facilitate healing.

- Other healing crystals for beginners are:

- Amethyst
- Clear quartz
- Quartz
- Citrine
- Black tourmaline
- Selenite

Protective crystals for beginners are:

- Black obsidian
- Smoky quartz
- Tiger's eye
- Red jasper

Pendulums

Pendulums can also contain crystals and work well when you bond with the pendulum by wearing it as a necklace. It is a tool used for divination work and focuses on YES/NO/MAYBE answers. A pendulum is symmetrical and evenly balanced. It should never be magnetic as this can skew the results. The power does not come from the pendulum itself, but rather it is a tool for you to channel psychic power through. Many people find this task difficult as it requires focus and identifying the miniscule changes in the movement of the pendulum.

Chromotherapy

Chromotherapy is a type of therapy using colour for healing heavily based on the chakra system and colours of the electromagnetic frequency scale -

ROY.G.BIV - Red, orange, yellow, green, blue, indigo and violet. This has been used for centuries and found to be effective in scientific studies (https://www.ncbi.nlm.nih.gov/pmc/articles/PMC1297510/) especially in saunas. Jaundiced babies receive blue light therapy to remedy the build up from the liver as it breaks down bilirubin. Light therapy is also used in swimming pools to kill bacteria and parasites alongside the chlorine.

Sacred Geometry and Mathematics

Within nature, there are patterns that can be seen across genus and species. Five patterns in nature have a Fibonacci sequence and it becomes a spiral; plants have different needs and therefore require a choice of leaf/petal patterns in order to thrive. The seeds of a sunflower are a great example of this.

The Fibonacci sequence is a set of recurring numbers that add up to make the following number and then use the last number to add up to the next number. Leonardo Pisano Bogollo noticed this pattern: 0, 1, 1, 2, 3, 5, 8, 13, 21, 34 etc.

Mathematically, the Greeks found that the golden ratio looks like a perfect rectangle, much like the Parthenon in Athens. Phi – 1.6 will continue with no distinct number pattern - 1.61803398874989484820 and so on. It is incredibly aesthetically pleasing to the eye which can be seen in architecture around the world.

This technique has been used throughout history and remains popular. Reiki is an alternative therapy originating in Japan. The Reiki practitioner or Master uses life force energy to heal your body. Some may use a light touch on appropriate body areas, or others hover their hands over. A good tool to start with is here: Reiki.org – What is Reiki?

The placebo effect has a substantial positive change in a person's mindset. A scientific study recently showed that Reiki is more effective than a placebo, which already transforms people. https://www.ncbi.nlm.nih.gov/pmc/articles/PMC5871310/

Clearing energies

When clearing energy, many people think of white sage, which has incredible cleansing properties. However, the indigenous people (Native Americans/First Nations) sage stocks had been devastated by white people. Therefore, the use of White Sage is a closed practice unless you are actively purchasing items or stock that directly support indigenous people. As a white person, I still would not use white sage to smudge; many impressive herbs are available and linked to the west, such as lavender. Please source items responsibly and ethically where financially possible if you cannot afford ethical things and educate yourself and others on these issues instead of a trade for the physical object. The system will not dismantle overnight and it requires conscious decision after conscious decision.

Incense sticks are a great way to cleanse your area by walking around with the incense stick, allowing the smoke to wash over the sites: you are a blessing and the sites will be too. You can also wave the incense stick around yourself like a halo to cleanse yourself of negative energies.

Cleaning with essential oils and words of affirmation can make for a beautiful space. But, a word of warning, essential oils can be detrimental to humans and animals. They must be adequately diluted and some are highly toxic to cats and dogs. I would advise against using them topically and please observe your pet when using diffusers incase of emergencies.

Peppermint around windows and doors can repel spiders. Make up a mix of peppermint essential oil and water, spray around the windows and doors, and make sure to dry it up with a paper towel. Usually, oils must be in a carrier oil, so please read the instructions and identify which type of oil you are purchasing.

Again, please conduct your own research. I have attached a small guide on suitable essential oils but please do monitor your pets and yourself if using essential oils as always, your mileage may vary.

Using "Are Essential Oils Safe for Dogs and Cats?", please see the guide below.

Essential Oils Safe for Dogs

- Cedarwood oil - acts as an insect repellant
- Chamomile oil - elicits a soothing effect and helps calm the gastrointestinal system
- Citrus oils (including lemon oil and orange oil): act as a mosquito repellant and deodoriser
- Eucalyptus oil
- Fennel oil
- Frankincense oil - currently being evaluated as a therapy for bladder cancer in humans and dogs
- Helichrysum oil - a member of the sunflower family with some potential in aiding bleeding disorders
- Lavender oil - induces a calming effect
- Lemongrass oil
- Certain mint oils (peppermint, spearmint) can help calm GI upset
- Rose oil

Essential Oils Safe for Cats

- Chamomile oil
- Jasmine oil

- Lavender oil
- Rose oil

Baths are incredibly healing. The hot water soothes aches and pains and you are lighter in the water, which takes the pressure off of muscles and joints. Some people find baths very relaxing to the point of falling asleep; please be very careful, especially if using candles and/or other substances.

A bath ritual that might be useful for you is as follows:

Before getting in the bath, make sure you have a glass of water at the side, the candles are in a safe position for burning, play some healing music – away from the bathwater, and use some Epsom salts in the bath water. If you are feeling fancy, feel free to add dried flowers or a bath bomb. Be wary of the active ingredients as some can disrupt the pH of the vulva and vagina, which results in discomfort and even yeast infections.

You can anoint your bathwater with one or two drops of essential oils such as lavender. In addition, people with skin conditions that are bacterial or fungal in nature may support their healing by adding 1-2 drops of pure tea tree oil in with the Epsom salts (please continue to seek the guidance of a health professional if you are unwell).

Showers are an excellent tool for cleansing. This is a great way to visualise all the negativity washing off you and heading down the drain. There is something so revitalising about a shower: you can dance and sing in there (slip hazard!) or cry your eyes out. Regardless, you are going to feel better afterwards. So create a shower playlist and see how it impacts your day.

Meditation

Often, when "meditation" comes to mind, images of people sitting quietly start flooding in. This is one way to meditate, but it does not meet everyone's needs, especially those of the neurodiverse.

Believed to have begun in India, spreading out over Asia, the origins are rooted in Hinduism and Buddhism. However, meditative practices can be seen in many religions. For example, in Islam, Muslims pray to Mecca five times a day, where they place their heads on the ground, very similar to child pose, an intensely healing yoga pose.

Yoga is a type of movement meditation. It has become incredibly westernised and expensive, and we must return yoga to its roots. It is used to bring awareness to the body and help the mind meet the body to have an excellent partnership.

When we are affected by trauma, or if the vasovagal nerve is disrupted, we don't get an appetite due to butterflies in the stomach which can then disrupt our biological processes. Practising Yoga allows you to recreate that connection. Yoga was never about super fancy poses or competition in the studio; you are there for yourself and your community. Finding the proper yoga studio for you will take some trial and error. Some studios will be more focused on Instagram etc., showing off challenging poses – but please do not be put off because there are plenty of classes for beginners. If you can find a trauma-informed yoga studio, then even better. There are lots of free YouTube channels for you to get started on. Yoga by Adriene is fabulous.

Another form of meditation is painting. Bob Ross was very zen. Focusing on something creative nourishes your soul. It doesn't matter if it is "good" or not. If you enjoyed the time you spent making or drawing something, then it is time well spent. It is easier to notice negative thought patterns when doing something like this, and you can nip that inner critic in the bud. You are constantly healing and evolving.

Again, reading or slow exercises such as swimming or Tai Chi bring awareness to the body and require deep breathing to do the movements.

Journaling

This doesn't have to be on paper, especially if you have dyslexia or another barrier to learning. An audio diary, online diary (word or notes) are great alternatives to writing things down. Text to speech is a great function too.

Journaling helps you identify what is going on deep in the psyche. Like doing maths, you show your working. Write about your feelings regarding a particular scenario, what happened, and what you want to focus on next time. It supports personal growth because you can identify your toxic traits or areas needing improvement, such as communication.

Remember to date your entries. Many people keep their old diaries and look back fondly on them. However, if you are going to keep them and some are NSFW, then protect your future self and label them so!

If you are dealing with toxic people, keeping a well-hidden diary is essential. Having a safe space to work out my mixed feelings stopped me from saying things I would regret and understand that most things were projected and never actually about me in the first place.

Guided meditations

Guided meditations are a great resource to help you relax. They also have a mix of binaural beats, healing frequencies and ASMR. Their purpose is to take your mind to a healing state, where it is receptive to growth and acceptance. Guided meditations with a voice narrator especially should not be done when driving or operating machinery; ideally, these are for downtime and before bed.

Past lives

Some children remember their past lives so vividly, and it impedes their current life. Children are open psychically because they have yet to be moulded by society and closed off their gifts. Spiritually, there is much to be learned from children and how they tap into their innate powers.

There are past life guided meditations available on YouTube that can be helpful when trying to access that part of your psyche. Similarly, you may want to see a past life psychic or experience hypnosis for a past life regression. Sometimes what comes up can be upsetting and having a practitioner on hand for support is helpful. Many have met a gruesome end or died in unfortunate circumstances, so it should be approached with caution. Do you have the necessary healthy coping mechanisms to manage what comes up? If not, how can you reach those goals so that you may eventually have a past life regression experience?

Ancestor work can be achieved through therapy, past life regressions and psychedelics. This is how many Indigenous people communicate with theirs, through rituals and ceremonies centred around gratitude and the power of plants.

Psychedelics

Magic Mushrooms and Truffles contain a naturally occurring substance called psilocybin. These psychedelics are found in nature in the form of fungi or plant matter. Ayahuasca's active ingredient is DMT which is also found in LSD. In the United Kingdom (2021), it is still currently a crime to be in possession of psilocybin, as they are Class A drugs. However, psilocybin is being used in clinical trials to assess the efficacy as a treatment for otherwise treatment-resistant depression.

The LD50 is the shorthand for “lethal dose” and lists substances that are non-toxic to severely toxic. Cannabis and Magic Mushrooms are the least toxic substances, whereas alcohol is closer in range to heroin and crack cocaine. For a person to overdose on cannabis, they would need to smoke 100,000 joints in a day.

There are indigenous magic mushroom species all over the world and they can pop in the United Kingdom during the cold mornings of Autumn. There are many mushrooms that are similar to the commonly found “liberty cap.” But please never ever pick a mushroom unless you are absolutely confident you can identify it. There are several lethal mushrooms and some that are incredibly toxic.

Mycologists will always advise foragers to take a spore print of the fungi and take a photo just after picking. A true liberty cap will look like it has a bruised stem which is blue purple, then disappears as it dries out. This trait is visible in other species which is why it is so crucial to properly identify them.

Tripping: What to expect and how to prepare

Disclaimer: This ebook does not encourage the use or sale of Class A drugs. This chapter is to educate and inform. YouTube has many resources from Eckhart Tolle and Alan Watt on psychedelics.

Safe spaces with sober sitters

Tripping in a familiar setting with a trusted sober friend is recommended. If at any point you feel too overwhelmed and want it to stop, eat something sugary. Having sweeties on hand will help mellow out the trip and raise your blood sugar, which can sometimes stop the impending doom from taking over your experience.

Consumption and onset

Eat a small breakfast or snack a few hours prior to tripping. An empty stomach is recommended because it can make people nauseous and allows the mushrooms to have a stronger impact as the psilocybin enters the bloodstream and moves through the blood brain barrier (BBB).

Oral consumption by chewing the matter into a paste and swallowing it to the stomach is common. Some people use a mortar and pestle to make gelatin capsules containing the truffles or mushrooms as this is far more gentle on the stomach. Symptoms that may occur after ingestion include nausea and vomiting. Some people are particularly sensitive and experience IBS symptoms too. Everyone is different, but a trip can last up to eight hours, depending on the amount of psilocybin consumed.

What to expect

Psilocybin can affect people differently. It is essential to note this and be prepared for any eventuality. Like most things, psilocybin trips are mind over matter, and a bad trip can occur when you get into a negative mindset. You begin to vibrate at a level of fear and soon that is all you feel. It is paramount to respect the plant you are eating and not be smug or arrogant. Equally, it would be best if you did not fear it as it can be the most beautiful life lesson.

The onset can be gradual. Most people report feeling “floaty” and start to see shimmering in daily objects that do not shimmer. Many feel euphoric, and it helps to have an upbeat playlist to listen to during this phase, as the urge to move about can be substantial. A magic mushroom experience is wonderful but intense. Your body feels warm and you may feel some tingling. Pink Floyd wrote Comfortably Numb, not about drugs necessarily but about freedom in childhood and how everything is a new experience. This is how a trip feels. Doing yoga whilst coming up helps maintain the link with your body and ground yourself during any uncomfortable moments that may arise. When you consume psychedelics, whether they are magic mushrooms, truffles, LSD or ayahuasca, do some research and preparation.

Trips can remove emotional blockages, repressed memories, and trauma, so you need to make sure that you want to do this. With knowledge, there is no going back. You know what you know, and sometimes you wish you didn't. The visual hallucinations can become quite solid and colourful. Breathe deeply when you are feeling overwhelmed. Similarly, auditory hallucinations can happen and can be drowned out by music if the person tripping feels uneasy.

There is a distinct afterglow from psilocybin use which many users compare to a system reboot. Many report feeling happier and lighter and more able to cope with difficult situations.

Microdosing for chronic illnesses

Microdosing psilocybin is becoming more common, particularly for chronic health conditions and mental health conditions such as treatment-resistant depression. Micro-dose amounts can vary from 25mg up to 75mg depending on height and weight. Generally, 3g of plant/fungi matter should be consumed for a spiritual trip to reach hallucinogenic states.

Why were they criminalised?

In the 1970s, Richard Nixon, the president of the United States of America, started a war on drugs and further segregation of white and black people. He associated people of colour with drugs such as heroin and cannabis, creating a false narrative. In this decade, magic mushrooms also became popular. People were very loving and open, spending time with one another, not money.

John Ehrlichman, a Nixon aide, admitted: *"You want to know what this was all about. The Nixon campaign in 1968, and the Nixon White House after that, had two enemies: the anti-war left and black people. We knew we couldn't make it illegal to be either against the war or black, but by getting the public to associate the hippies with marijuana and blacks with heroin, and then criminalising both heavily, we could disrupt those communities.* Here, the aide admits the racial motivation behind 'the war on drugs'. He continued discussing their blatant disregard for human rights , *"We could arrest their leaders, raid their homes, break up their meetings, and vilify them night after night on the evening news. Did we know we were lying about the drugs? Of course, we did."*

If we look at the LD50, which is the lethal dose due to toxicity, we can see the disparity between psychedelics and opiates. Why are hallucinogens and psychedelics considered so dangerous when they are at the very bottom of the scale? Alcohol is more toxic to the human body than magic mushrooms or cannabis. Another reason that psychedelics are banned and criminalised is that they allow people to reach higher consciousness and awaken to the fact that we do not need to run the rat race. Psilocybin helps us think critically and see things from a different perspective. In terms of compliance, this is what the government does not want.

In summary, psilocybin is the least toxic psychoactive drug on the LD50 scale. However, non-toxicity and intolerances or allergies are not the same thing. Always approach drugs with caution.
Psilocybin is an indigenous medicine to those in countries where they are viable. Liberty Caps for example are the most common type found in Scotland.

DMT

DMT or dimethyltryptamine is thought to be produced by the pineal gland and the brain during such times as dreaming, birth and death, and near-death experiences. It is the active ingredient in the Ayahuasca brew and produces similar results to psychedelics. It is naturally occurring and can also be made in a laboratory. Some people find this experience very unsettling as it can be pretty intense. DMT comes in the form of a white powder which can be smoked, vaporised or snorted. In religious ceremonies and indigenous practises, the plants are boiled to make a tea which is then consumed. The plant-based tea has a slower onset than lab-made DMT, which can be felt between 5 to 10 minutes.

Ayahuasca trips can last up to six hours. Whereas synthetic DMT can last up to an hour. There are more increased risks with DMT consumption and it is higher on the scale LD50. In extremely rare cases, some people may experience persistent psychosis or hallucinogen persisting perception disorder, which is more likely to be found in people with pre-existing mental health conditions.

If consuming psychedelics and hallucinogens, do not mix them with antidepressants as this can cause serotonin syndrome. DMT, in particular, should not be combined with alcohol, antihistamines, opioids, or any substance that is a "downer." Ideally, it should not be used in conjunction with any other substance for safe use at all.

We are currently cutting down Ayahuasca vines at an increasing rate, which is affecting the amount and quality of vine found on indigenous lands. It is being harvested faster that it can grow and nature is not being left to do its work. For people who buy their vines, the prices are increasing vastly. It is capitalism at its finest; supply and demand. We must plant more Ayahuasca if the species is to survive.

In South America, places such as Peru offer Ayahuasca ceremonies. If you do choose to attend a ceremony, please ensure the following:

- You are aware of the cultural differences and will attempt to learn basic Spanish
- You support indigenous people and their businesses
- You are critical of any white tourism that prospers off the back of colonialism and gentrification
- Most of these places are not luxurious and come with their own risks of travelling
- Be prepared for your body to purge physically and emotionally, which requires appropriate hygiene measures and mental health support

"*If you get the message, hang up the phone. For psychedelic drugs are simply instruments, like microscopes, telescopes, and telephones. The biologist does not sit with eye permanently glued to the microscope; he goes away and works on what he has seen."* - Alan Watts.

It is crucial not to depend on psychedelics for inner work and self-improvement, as it is a tool which, like most things, can be abused. Psilocybin tolerance spikes after immediate use, meaning you will be unlikely to trip the following day on the same amount consumed the day before.

It is important not to rely on trips purely for escapism because we are supposed to have one foot in the physical realm. Being grounded enough to experience and learn the lessons from the plants are crucial.

Talking to plants

Plants are medicine and have a vibration, we should talk to them.

The great, great granddaughter of Charles Darwin, esteemed biologist and evolutionist, took part in an experiment where participants had to talk to plants. The experiment relates back to one of Darwin's theories where plants are affected by vibration, which is true now that we know everything in the universe has a vibration. Ms Darwin's tomato plant was the largest, she had read her ancestor;s "Origin of Species" to the tomato plant.

Mythbusters tried this experiment and found that music helped the plants grow in comparison to the control plants that did not receive any communication or music. It seems the plants respond well to women's voices but this could be in correlation to the tone and pitch of their voice.

Kambo Practices

The giant monkey frog, also known as Phyllomedusa Bicolour, produces poisonous secretions to ward off predators. This has been used as a potent healing practice in indigenous cultures in the Amazon rainforest.

Firstly, minor wounds to the skin are made to open a barrier. Then the frog secretion is applied in a small amount on top of these minor abrasions.

Kambo is used for purging and many of these symptoms have a quick onset. Before applying the frog toxin, a practitioner will ask you to consume about a litre of water to prepare you for the purging, which often comes in the form of sickness and diarrhoea. It can also cause intense sweating and emotional responses such as crying. Afterwards, the client needs to rehydrate by drinking water or tea; however, no more than a litre and a half.

A first-time client should only have a small dose to assist the individual and their tolerance. This toxin is used to shock the system and offer a reboot through the pharmacological effects from the act of neuropeptides found in the Kambo. Rehydration should be monitored; in rare cases, there can be a syndrome of inappropriate antidiuretic hormone secretion.

Kambo is not a psychoactive or hallucinogenic substance.

Ethical Cacao

Cacao is naturally serotonergic in nature, it should not be consumed if the individual is on SSRIs or MAOIs.

Cacao ceremonies are common in Mesoamerican cultures. The Mayans first consumed chocolate in the form of cacao, which grows on trees. Cocoa was a typo, misspelling from Mayan to English during trade. The Aztecs conquered the Mayans and loved the Cacao which was consumed in the form of a hot drink, adding chili to it. Chilli's bring enhance the natural flavour in the chocolate. White chocolate is not a proper chocolate as it does not contain cacao.

It was used for social gatherings as a way to raise spirits but the beans were also a form of currency. Cacao was used as a form of medicine and treated conditions such as fainting.

The Maya drank chocolate as a frothy, hot, bitter drink which was prepared by pouring the liquids into other vials from a great height, back and forth, until a frothy layer appeared. The steps were:

1. Mix the cacao paste with water
2. Add spices such as chilli peppers and cornmeal
3. Pour the concoction back and forth from cup to pot until it develops thick foam on top
4. Sweeten with honey or flower nectar

Cacao ceremonies with others encourage a shared experience and can raise vibrations. Everyone is on the same page and this manifests as they share the beverage over communication, singing and breathwork. Cacao is not psychoactive.

100% ethical cacao, produced from start to finish by GuateMayans, can be found here: https://snehasacred.com/store

Cacao was originally colonised by the Spanish when they invaded South American countries such as Peru, and it is important to acknowledge the suffering that was and is affecting the indigenous people from which these ceremonies came. Please ensure your money is going to the communities and indigenous people and not white people who profit from a false sense of spirituality. It is essential they receive reparations.

Rapé snuff

Rapé snuff is like a medicinal tobacco but it is not the same species that is used in modern cigarettes. Nicotiana Rustica is not smoked but inhaled through the nostrils. It should not be smoked because of the other medicinal properties that the plant holds. The snuff can also hold a mix of other medicines that are at the discretion of the Shaman. Rapé is psychotropic but not psychedelic.

The shaman or practitioner blows through the clients' nose using a v-shaped bamboo/bone pipe called a tepi pipe. It is blown forcefully in small amounts through each nostril and promotes alertness yet a calm demeanour. Indigenous peoples would often use Rapé before hunting to heighten their senses. Some people can vomit and the need for a bowel movement can be sudden. Rapé is said to purify the immune system. It is also a useful medicine for setting intentions as the client feels grounded yet aware.

Chapter Six - Signs From Spirit

Signs from spirit come in many different shapes and forms. Once you are open to the fact you receive messages from the Universe daily, and can ask for your own specific signs, things are gonna get wild!

Dr. Carder Stout puts it beautifully:

"Nothing happens by accident when your soul gets involved. It is the most intentional presence in your life whether you recognize its existence or not. Your soul is omniscient and ever present. It informs your decision making through the thoughts and images it provides. It is the essence that fuels your intuition. When you are certain of something it is your soul's voice that resounds from the depths of the psyche. When a mysterious coincidence occurs it is often the design of your soul's whimsical nature. Yes, the soul has a sense of humour and often speaks to us through metaphors, symbols, riddles, and clues. These hints require our full investigation in order to uncover their meaning."

Dr Stout is referring to the voice that feels like it's at the very back of the brain. It's the really deep part that is hard to grasp, like a fading dream once you've properly woken up. Sometimes it's clear as a bell and sometimes harder to understand. This is where signs from spirit come in.

Coincidence

"Coincidence awareness emerges through its spontaneous appearance in everyday life. Rather than removing you from the events of daily life, coincidence awareness immerses you more deeply into your current life and then beyond" - Bernard D. Beitman M.D.

Connecting with Coincidence

"Coincidence means only a connection that's not seen. Roots meet underground" – Charlotte Armstrong.

DejaVu

This is a sign that your third eye and crown chakras are developing well. You are identifying that you've experienced this before and the Universe is telling you that you are on the correct path.

There are a few theories as to what Deja Vu is, and I think they all can apply in different scenarios.

1. This could be a past life experience and you are witnessing a regression

2. Your energy matches the environment or person at that moment in time (also, the right moment at the right time)
3. Ancestral traumas are rising to the surface for emotional healing
4. You foresaw this moment in a dream or a vision

Feathers

I often see feathers on the ground or floating down in the air. Some have had them blown in the window or brought back as a gift by their child or pet. Can you think of a time where you crossed paths with a feather? What were you thinking about at the time?

White

A white feather signifies spiritual protection and divine guidance that you are on the correct path. This can also be a sign that your loved ones who have departed the physical realm, are happy and well.

Black

Your magic is accessible within. This is another sign you are strongly protected by the Universe and your loved ones.

Red

Red feathers represent the life force and vitality of the Universe. This could signify you are gaining strength or even overcoming a health issue.

Yellow

Yellow feathers are a reminder of our freedoms and joy and to stay grateful for our manifestations. It can also represent a bright future ahead if it appears to someone who is feeling hopeless or in despair.

Orange

Orange represents creativity and emotional balance. It is also a sign that it's time to manifest! It can also mean some love is entering your life too.

Blue

The Universe is hearing your wishes and manifestations, they are coming to fruition. This can also be a reminder to listen.

Green

Abundance in the form of money! Success in finances, life and love.

Purple

Purple deeply represents psychic abilities and intuition, so this is a sign that these gifts are opening up for you. It can also be a sign you are actively transmuting negative energies into something positive or manipulating something to work in your favour, when it initially was used against you.

Grey

Grey feathers represent neutrality. They ask for calmness and request peace.

"*Why do birds suddenly appear, everytime you are near? Just like me, they long to be, close to you*" – The Carpenters.

Animals and insects appearing around you is another positive sign that you are attracting higher frequencies. Animals and insects are innocent beings and often mean us no harm unless provoked or psychologically tortured. In my opinion, this is why it is critical to rescue dogs and other pets and give them the love, the time and the lessons required to live a happy life; they didn't deserve to be abused.

You may or may not turn into a real life Snow White, but be aware of the other beings in your life that are attracted to you.

Electronic disturbances

Have you ever had an eerie experience where you talk about something spiritual or a departed loved one, then the lights start flickering? Yes, this is spirit communicating too! It can happen on the daily for some people, to the point they hire an electrician to inspect the wiring inside their house. Spirit uses the energy from electronics to make contact, as it requires a great deal of energy. This is also why mediums and channelling psychics are often exhausted after conversing with spirit.

Other people

Sometimes the Universe brings us into contact with someone on a specific day so that they give us a certain message, or we overhear something that sets our wheels in motion. Other times, we actively seek out messages which is why many individuals see psychics.

Numbers

Repeating numbers on license plates, social media, wherever you see them – they are a sign! Please refer to the earlier chapter in Astrology to work out the numerology behind the numbers you are observing. It's a coded message just for you.

Lyrics in songs

Have you ever sat in the car, turned the radio on, you are going through a break-up and some ridiculous love song comes on, and you just sob? Sound familiar? The Universe gives us cues and reminds us to feel our feelings. It's ok to feel hurt and want to cry.

There is a spoken word poem on the track "Good Life" – By ZHU, and each time I listen to it, I learn something new or am prompted to use a different perspective. What song does this for you?

[Note for audio artist, listen to the song to get the flow, it's really good!]

"Gratitude is my destination
My destiny is perfectly aligned with this location
I am the map, so I travel back in time
I have everything I want cause my imagination is mine
But mind is not enough for me cause I am not my mind
I could see it all, but never get to see I'm truly blind
I could be it all, but all identities intertwine
The moon is only bright cause it reflects the sun's shine"

This song represents the answers that we have in ourselves. It tells the story of someone who is aware that they are the universe experiencing itself. They are aware they will never know everything or get to experience everything and accept this.

Music saves lives. How many times has a fan expressed this to an artist? I have seen so many young people triumph over horrendous adversities by throwing themselves into music. Sometimes you do feel as though a song was written especially for you, or about your situation – and that is a sign from the Universe!

I shuffle my music on the app multiple times a day, asking questions and observing the answers.

Literal signs

Seeing a word on the side of a bus or on a billboard. This is a direct communication from the Universe. It could be a poster on the subway or a headline in the paper that catches your eye.

Dreams

Repeating dreams are trying to tell you something. Whether they are pleasant in nature or nightmarish, journaling is a great way to establish what is going on in the depths of your psyche. For example, a dream about losing teeth is usually a sign of anxiety and stress. A dream diary is the best way to get the most out of your dreams, by immediately writing down what happened upon waking.

Random thoughts

Sometimes a random thought hits us out of nowhere, about something totally irrelevant to the task at hand. This is divine inspiration. Sometimes the clarity comes many moons later and it suddenly hits us, or we get the solution to a problem suddenly.

Bugs and insects

Spiders are said to be seen as helpful spirits because they keep lesser creatures out of the home. They represent protection and creativity due to the intricate webs they weave. Certain threads of the web have alarm bells, just like the human body has an internal security system. Seeing spiders can also indicate you are deeply connected spiritually and are at the centre of your web, a metaphor for being in alignment.

Lady Bugs are fortuitous beetles and depict some positivity heading your way. The Lady Bug has a beautiful red shell often adorned with black dots. They bring news of good fortune and luck. They also represent transformation due to their life cycle, beginning as a larvae, then forming into a hard-shelled colourful being.

A Butterfly is another insect of transformation and the sight of one may indicate your transformation and what you have been through, or a wonderful transformation is to come.

The Dragonfly signifies change, ever moving and an insect with one of the shortest life cycles, they know how to live it up! They breed in water and then move to the air; Dragonflies are incredibly adaptable.

Birds

The Owl is depicted in many cultures as a wise, knowing creature. This bird insinuates a deep connection to the knowledge of the Universe. They also describe higher intuition and the ability to see beyond illusions.

The Bald Eagle has mighty wings and soars through the sky, it is rare for it to be taken down by another predator. They have strong legs and large talons to navigate the Earth and Water habitats when looking for food. They describe freedom and the ability to look ahead and Native Americans have labelled the Eagle as a symbol of wisdom and hope. The Eagle manages the balance of life, by picking weak or sick prey, thus removing their genes from the pool of reproduction and strengthening the species.

The Raven is closely related to magick and this means great changes can be achieved. The Raven encourages you to work with your shadow-self and heal. The sight of a Raven can reveal some uncomfortable truths, but this will aid your journey in the long run. The Raven reminds you that although there is darkness, there is also light, and we need both to maintain balance.

The Hummingbird has a rapid heart-rate, pushing blood around the body to satisfy the great needs of its lightning fast wings. Although they are small, Hummingbirds can in fact fly long distances during migration, over a thousand miles! They also have the ability to fly backwards. Spiritually, they signify optimism and positivity, enjoying your life.

Common Mammals

A Rabbit can mean a few things depending on the culture. A Rabbit's foot was originally used as a good luck charm, but for some it can mean anxiety and timidness. This could refer to a person who is intelligent and they are working to overcome their social anxieties.

Foxes are known to be tricky but they also have an incredibly intelligent side. Foxes are cunning and have great problem solving abilities. They are quick thinkers and super responsive. The Fox can mean you are improving these qualities and are able to cut through the fluff. They are also nocturnal mammals so this may indicate an affinity for the night if you see them often.

The Cat is an animal that has high boundaries. Unlike Dogs, they are very selective about where and who they spend their time with. Cats are fiercely independent, but do enjoy company if it brings them something. Cats can see incredibly well in the dark, and were revered in Ancient Egypt for their nocturnal sight. Black Cats crossing your path are positive omens, not negative. There is a disparity in animals with black fur in comparison with other colours in terms of animal adoption. Black Cats are beautiful and remind us we have a foot in the physical realm and the spirit realm.

A Deer sighting signifies that you are a sensitive soul and are highly intuitive. You are graceful yet intimidating, people know to approach you slowly and with ease. Deer are seen as very gentle beings and can bolt in many different directions, meaning they are adaptable. In the winter, for some Stags, their antlers shed the skin which looks like a mass murder has taken place, as the velvet that surrounds their bone is incredibly vascular. You too can shed your skin and grow.

Spirit Animals

Indigenous people and shamans have taught us that animals are here to guide us, with some animals being deeply connected to humans. The animal chooses the person. This is deeply sacred in traditional Native American culture.

Have you felt drawn to a particular animal and was never really sure why?

Are there any animals that show up in your life, or at major events?

What animal are you afraid of?

To access this part of your spirituality, reflection and journaling will be required. Please be wary of appropriation of the culture, phrases such as "dolphins are my spirit animal" because they like dolphins and for no other reason, are damaging and dilute the true meaning to its people.

Seeing people who look like the person you are thinking of

Sometimes when we are thinking of someone, or they are about to get in contact with us - we start to see people who look like them. It sounds really bizarre but doppelgangers come out of the woodwork, people with similar phrases or banter come into earshot; these are all signs from the universe that communication should be opening up. They also may be thinking of you very intensely to bring about these changes in the physical realm.

Seeing orbs

Orbs are balls of light which can be captured on camera or seen with the naked eye. Mostly they are said to be departed loved ones or angels, offering their love and protection. They can come in different colours, much like the chakra system.

Chapter Seven - Occultism

The occult, not to be mistaken for yakult (the yoghurt), has been a practice that has stood the test of time, passed down for centuries. “Occult” is latin for “hidden” , essentially hidden knowledge. Our ancestors put knowledge above all; monetary greed is a relatively new concept and corruption is at an all time high.

J.P. Morgan said, “millionaires don’t use astrology, the billionaires do.” You can use these ancient occult practices to better yourself and attract the abundance desired. It’s vital for empaths and highly sensitive people to find a practice they align with, but most importantly just to have an outlet and a channel for the divine.

Whether you define yourself as a witch or goddess/god, believing in yourself is the critical part. The tools are just that: tools. The power is within, cliche as it sounds.

There are many realms and dimensions to explore, levels of consciousness and experiences to be had. This chapter will explain how to access the spirit world safely, following on from the protective chapter to ensure you can do this safely.

You can create a spell for pretty much anything. In fact, many online resources talk through the ingredients for specific things, but the main ingredient is intention. You can have all the ingredients globally, but it needs to have a purpose or a goal. Write down what your desired destination/goal is from creating and casting your spell.

I do not recommend making love spells, curses or hex jars. Interrupting or trying to control someone else's freedom will always end up backfiring, in my opinion. Making someone who doesn't love you be your person, is manipulative. That is not real love.

Voodoo and Hoodoo (particularly the former) are closed practices and have different cultural approaches to magick. The magick is deeply rooted in the deep south and New Orleans, heavily based on ancestor worship and control of meddling spirits. There is a large community and it is considered a folk magick.

Earlier we touched on veganism and the colonial approach to animals. Similarly, in Voodoo and Hoodoo, sacrifices are made with animals. This has been a long standing ritual within ceremonies for hundreds of years.

If you are a white person who is actively working to be anti-racist, you have nothing to fear from Voodoo and Hoodoo practitioners. People tend to fear what they do not understand. Saying this, however, I would recommend not practicing Voodoo and Hoodoo unless you are a part of the community; the same goes as well for copying indiginous practices. If you are not a part of these historic communities or do not have family or ancestry in those communities, they are not your communities to take practices or resources from.

With the state of the meat industry there is no leg to stand on, as they say "people who live in glass houses don't throw stones". Similarly this bible passage Matthew 7:1-3: "*Do not judge, so that you may not be judged. For with the judgment you make you will be judged, and the measure you give will be the measure you get."*

Some use the term witch and actively practice witchcraft, this is not associated with a religion or 'good' and 'evil'. Witches use the energy available to them and are committed to lifelong learning, which is recorded in a sacred book called a Grimoire.

Witch's familiar

European folklore states that some witches have a familiar, usually in the form of a household pet. They can appear as amphibians, reptiles, insects and arachnids. During the medieval witch hunts, a witch would have her body searched for 'teats' which could be anything from a supernumerary nipple to warts and skin tags. This is apparently how the witch would feed her familiar.

Familiars are here to protect us and provide company. Many people have pets who are so sensitive to psychic phenomena. We also use dogs for medical support, their sensitive noses can identify when a seizure is imminent or their owner is reaching a hypoglycemic state.

We have walked with animals for millenia, we can have a symbiotic relationship with them if we can care for them and the Earth appropriately.

Before modern times of choosing a pet, a familiar would appear to a witch and then stay with her. However, a call can be placed to the universe to bring one into her life. I enjoy Phillip Pullman's description of the witches daemon in his books 'The Amber Spyglass' and 'The Subtle Knife', following on from 'The Golden Compass'. This trilogy is multidimensional and although fictional, discusses aspects of the soul. They were amazing books to read as a young adult. Terry Pratchett's 'A hat full of sky' is also an interesting read. A fictional witch gets her body hijacked and must get it back, which is why we protect ourselves people!

Yoga Nidra

Yoga Nidra is a type of meditation that is very intense and can support lucid dreaming. This is different from travelling the astral plane, because you are dreaming deeply in the subconscious. You can control the dream and the environment. On the astral plane, you are still on Earth and bound by certain laws of physics. Fair warning, it can bring on wild and colourful dreams, possibly even awaken past traumas that must arise to be healed. It can also be a "noisy" meditation due to the instruments used, again this depends on the type of Yoga Nidra meditation you have selected.

My personal experiences are: feeling as though I am walking through mud. There is so much resistance when I try to move. I had woken in my kitchen and knew I was not in reality. I felt a little uneasy, so I got up to return to my body which was in the bedroom. I slowly waded over but banged into the doorway (which is something I often do in my physical body), which snapped me awake physically. Another time, I was becoming aware that I had been travelling and had returned to my body. Again, I felt this resistance, almost like a G-Force dragging the air all around me. I slowly came to and realised what was happening. It is quite a personal experience. There is much anecdotal evidence online if you would like to hear other peoples stories.

Yoga Nidra can be a segue into travelling the astral plane.

Travelling the astral plane

There are five types of body that we each have. The physical body is what we are in on a day to day basis, when we sleep or have out-of-body experiences, our etheric body, which looks like us physically, explores. This generally happens when we are sleeping, and some people recall travelling once they've woken. Others don't realise they are doing it and aren't aware of lucid dreaming.

Creating a totem or having a jar of sand in the room will help ground you and remain tethered to your body, as the sudden snapback can be somewhat disorientating. Imagine it like spiritual whiplash.

Ouija boards

Ouija boards are direct lines to spirit but can be incredibly dangerous. I usually do not allow fear to envelop me, but this practice must be done with the utmost care. You must only place one finger lightly on the planchette otherwise you could unknowingly push it around yourself, it is really easy to succumb to the fear and hysteria especially if this is performed in a group setting.

As always, cleanse and protect the space before beginning any work whereby you try to contact people not in this dimension. You are responsible.

To protect yourself if you wish to use Ouija boards, there are several important rules to follow:

- Never do an Ouija board in any participant's home; the memories and emotions of this person are deeply linked to their home and can be ripe for an attachment
- Do not do it alone. If you must undertake this, please do it in an area that doesn't mean anything to you
- Open and close the practice using candles and setting intentions.
- Have sea salt available and a glass beside the board that is empty of liquid, this is like an emergency exit button
- If things become severe or frightening, smash the glass immediately (and as safely as possible) to cut the communication.
- Cleanse all negative energies after the Ouija board and do a full body scan to check in with how you are feeling. Better yet take a shower or a bath to physically cleanse any attachments that may have formed.

Working on Telepathy

In nature, telepathy is innate to some species such as ants and fungi. Individual ants make up a colony and share a hive mind: they work together as a collective, yet each ant has a job or a role. This hierarchy is not controlled by one being, but rather are a series of behavioural responses to chemicals known as pheromones. This chemical expression is a form of communication.

Similarly, fungi communicate with each other through a stringy network of mycelium, without ever saying a word. In conclusion, there is more than one way to communicate.

I'm sure you've heard of twin telepathy, but it is also common to be able to share thoughts with close loved ones whether they are platonic relationships, familial, or romantic. This usually manifests as people saying the same thing at the exact same time. It is also more than just words and phrases, many twins or close siblings can identify when their sibling is in pain or distressed. Meditating together can help open the telepathic link between two people.

Practice by sending telepathic images that you find easy enough to hold in your mind. It could be song lyrics, whatever works for you. Practice sending it out like an email or an energy field, again this is your imagination's chance to run wild.

In public, you could also attempt to gain strangers' attention or watch their reactions by pulling on a silver cord attached to them like a marionette. Imagining yourself as a broadcasting tower will help you messages be sent and received.

You can also improve intuition by laying Tarot cards out and trying to pick out the Major Arcana only.

Working with Deities

Deity work is not innate to witchcraft and is seen across multiple religions and cultures such as paganism. In Mexico, el día de los Muertos is celebrated on the first of November, after the celtic holiday Samhain also known as All Hallows Eve and Halloween.

During this time the veil between dimensions is thin and we are likely to have more contact and signs from ancestors and deities.

It is important to note not everyone will work with a deity or should do so. It is advanced and the practice is not to be taken lightly.

Working with a deity or deities requires the understanding that you are entering into a working relationship. This is different from worshipping a deity where gifts or prayers are left for them. You can call on them for support in spell work amongst other things, but this can be transactional. Avoid making deals until you know without a doubt who you are working with.

The worship part of deity work asks for a clean altar that is tended to often. Earlier in the book we touched on ‘pouring one out’, this is a great practice for deity work as many people leave food and drink out for the gods and goddesses. Use your common sense here. If you live in a hot country leaving food out will attract flies and roaches so perhaps candles and flowers would be a better choice. In colder climates, food and drinks can be left out. Many people tend to consume them the following day or bury the gifts in the earth, as long as you don’t bin the stuff if you can help it. If you struggle to organise yourself at the best of times, it may be better to avoid this approach as to not invoke the gods wrath.

Some individuals are chosen by their deity because they have a lesson to learn, or require support in their spiritual endeavours. You could be called to live at a different level from your peers because your soul has shit to do. This does not make you superior, but this level does come with great responsibility.

Signs you are being chosen:

Hades, Loki or the Morrigan all send signs through birds such as, seeing crows and ravens constantly and interacting with them. You will also feel a shift in energy which you pick up on either internally or externally, for example the atmosphere in the room feels heavier or cold.

Asking for a confirmation verbally and then research the deity to see if it resonates, repeating it like you would in a science experiment. If the deity can confirm the same sign, three times, thats usually a confirmation. However, it's wise to have another form of confirmation, perhaps through oracle cards or a reading from another practitioner.

What are tricksters?

An entity that displays intellect or has specific knowledge which it uses to defy human rules and behaviours. A well known trickster is Loki, a Norse entity able to shape-shift amongst other talents. He is the god of trickery and mischief.

A trickster does not have malicious intent for physical harm but they do thrive on drama and Chaos. Loki often masquerades as Thor and Odin, which is why it's vital to check and confirm who you are working with to avoid nasty surprises.

Follow your gut and intuition. If something feels off, it usually is.

Goddesses and Gods

Godesses and Gods are powerful beings, choosing to work with them is knowing that they are lending you their energy, and there is always a price and a consequence here in the physical. It takes a lot of energy to bring about change in our realm.

They have their own ideas and plans, lightness and darkness within, so do remember this when working with deities. They are unlikely to stay with you your entire life and may exit and re-enter several times. If you want to close down the relationship for whatever reason, make sure you practice gratitude and make it clear why it's ending. You could write them a letter, leave it on your altar then burn it the next day.

It is crucial to research the deity. There is a lot of information out there and you must discern what works best for you and your budget in terms of gifts or worship. If you are in the process of attracting money, take some fallen flowers from the garden for the altar. It's all about the intention. They like to see the effort of time and research. Different gods have different tastes and it can be surprising!

Goddesses and Gods you may be familiar with are Zeus, Artemis, Venus, Hermes, Medusa and Hades

Gods from Ancient Greece, Rome and Egypt are widely revered and celebrated. Ancient Roman and Greek deities tend to be similar but can have different energies. Diana is also known as Artemis in Ancient Greek mythology for example.

Angels and Demons

These tend to be 'demonised' for lack of a better word through the lens of Christianity. There is light and dark throughout the Universe, when these types of deities want to work with you it does not mean you are inherently good or evil. Some work with your shadow and some with your higher self.

It is important to note here that if you suffer with mental illness and are prone to hallucinations, please seek out help and support before assuming it is deity work. Mental illness is very real and it is easy to fall into delusion, especially if you are neurodiverse or have suffered trauma. Not all psychological presentations are spiritual, they can be very real symptoms for simple things like dehydration and lack of sleep amongst other things.

Demon has roots in Ancient Greece, where daemons (day-monn) were considered the bridge betweens the Gods of Olympus and humans on Earth. They were known as demi-gods or lesser gods and were known to favour humans.

As centuries passed, societies thought that demons were ancestors who had passed on but continued to watch over them. Then the myth of angels and demons were born from the belief, a daemon on each shoulder is an ancestor to guide us during difficult times that requires a hard choice to be made.

The New Testament described possessions, fallen angels banished from heaven, particularly Lucifer Morningstar who became Satan. Christianity interpreted that fallen angels are demons who rebelled against God thus leading to them being

thrown from the heavens as detailed in (Rev 12:7-9). Some christians believe that demons are the spawn of a human woman and an angel (Gen 6:2, Jude 1:6)
https://www3.dbu.edu/mitchell/biblical.htm

Satan is the word for adversary, and is God's nemesis. "Satan and his angels rebelled against God in heaven, and proudly presumed to try their strength with his. And when God, by his almighty power, overcame the strength of Satan, and sent him like lightning from heaven to hell with all his army; Satan still hoped to get the victory by subtlety" - https://books.google.co.uk/books?id=m3EAAAAAMAAJ&pg=PA87&redir_esc=y#v=onepage&q&f=false

I think there are two sides to every story, and from what I have researched about the Satanic Church, it seems very positive and progressive. The Satanic Church or Temple as it's also known is both liberal and humanist. The first tenet of seven is: "One should strive to act with compassion and empathy towards all creatures in accordance with reason."

In an interview with the Guardian Newspaper,, about the Satanic Church Lucian Greaves said: "The metaphor of Satan is just as important to a lot of us as it would be to anybody who takes it literally because we grew up in a Judaeo-Christian culture. It really does speak to us in a very pointed and poignant way about our place in our culture and what our affirmative values are … and, of course, it defines what we oppose: these kinds of theocratic norms and authoritarian structures."

The Satanic Church appears to act with more compassion than some churches in the branches of Christianity such as the Notorious Westboro Baptist Church. The Satanic Temple is pro LGBTQIA+ as stated in 'Hail Satan?' a documentary by Penny Lane about satanists. The Temple in the film is not associated with the Church of Satan, founded in 1966.

https://www.out.com/activism/2019/8/24/satanic-temple-says-it-will-fight-death-lbgtq-rights
https://www.theguardian.com/film/2019/aug/15/hail-satan-are-satanists-now-the-good-guys-in-the-fight-against-the-evangelical-right

The biblical figure King Solomon awoke with ten rings upon ten fingers the proof of a wise man recognized by God. Those rings came to be known as the Rings of Solomon, the "source of the magic that employs angels and demons." He became the ruler of the seven princes of hell which are correlated to the seven deadly sins: pride, lust, gluttony, sloth, greed, wrath and envy.

https://the-demonic-paradise.fandom.com/wiki/King_Solomon

Angelic or demonic deities are different from parasitic entities that attach themselves to you if you aren't protected spiritually or don't use the ouija board properly.

Parasitic Entities

We have all seen horror films that have ghosts, poltergeists and evil spirits. 'The Exorcist' film really set the precedent for ghost stories and is notorious in pop culture. Although incredibly rare and usually not as severe as portrayed in film, this can happen to individuals. There are tv shows that have ghost hunters go into people's homes who are at the end of their tether after being haunted, which is a terrifying experience.

Ghost hunters or paranormal investigators tend to have a lot of equipment on them when out in the field. They need specific instruments to pick up the subtle changes around us since spirits tend to be invisible. I will discuss shadow beings shortly after. Spirits use the electromagnetic spectrum like humans in the physical realm and draw energy from technology to act out here in this dimension. This takes a great deal of energy which sometimes causes cameras to break.

There are motion sensor cameras which work well and also cameras that snap a photo if the temperature changes as there is usually a drop in temperature. People who work with spirit usually report feeling cold or the air in the room being cold.

Many investigators use microphones to catch any whispers, footsteps or small noises that would otherwise go unnoticed. Some even use a tool called a spirit box which is designed to catch electronic voice phenomena and make it understandable. There are also computer programs that pick up movement and show where the spirit is, which is quite interesting, there are a few youtube channels that do ghost compilations with all the different tech.

Some young people have had spooky interactions on social media platforms like snapchat and instagram, picking up on faces behind them. The digital age allows us to capture psychic phenomena that would otherwise be thrown out as hysterical or disregarded by the scientific community. There are now heaps of sites, youtube channels and tv series dedicated to ghost hunting and paranormal investigations. As science progresses I imagine we will see more and more proof of the spirit world.

As time went on and the capitalist wheel began to turn, blessed items, blessings and exorcisms became monetised and services became prescribed rather than sought out. Churches don't pay tax and this became a lucrative business in some sects of christianity. Many exorcisms were performed for demonic possession when the true diagnosis for the patient was a brain tumour pressing into the frontal lobe causing severe personality changes. This is why it is essential to seek out qualified doctors as well as spiritual practitioners, as western medicine and homeopathy can have a symbiotic relationship.

https://www.washingtonpost.com/posteverything/wp/2016/07/01/as-a-psychiatrist-i-diagnose-mental-illness-and-sometimes-demonic-possession/

An article in the Washing Post covered a Psychiatrist's journey into the occult, where they help diagnose who is suffering from mental illness and who is experiencing a demonic possession. Dr Richard Gallagher has spent two decades distinguishing between the two.

Signs of demonic possession include:

- Trouble sleeping - This can be more than bouts of insomnia, more of a fear of sleeping or fearing their dreams. The person may also suffer from sleep paralysis.
- Having and sharing hidden knowledge such as intimate details of people in the room or other information that the person couldn't possibly know.
- Bouts of extreme strength
- Extreme personality change so far removed from their normal self
- Shouting profanities and speaking in other languages previously unknown to them
- There have been anecdotal accounts of levitations but this phenomenon is both bizarre and rare.

They attach by:

- Seeking vulnerable people such as empaths of sensitive people that are spiritually open and unprotected. They will also try people who are suffering from addiction.

- Entering this realm via poor spiritual practices on the practitioner's behalf, not cleansing the space or using the ouija board properly are good examples.
- A healer accidentally takes on the entity because they have left themselves spiritually open after performing reiki. It is vital for healers to take some personal time between clients.

They are removed by:

- Upkeep of good spiritual hygiene as mentioned earlier in the book. Using crystals such as tourmaline and obsidian for protection and selenite for healing.
- Seeking out help from someone trained in banishing if you are not christian or disagree with exorcism practices.
- Christian items such as the holy cross, holy water and the bible will draw out the entity.
- Positive affirmations and intentions said to oneself and told by others to build up their spiritual immune system.
- Healing circles as long as your peers are equipped to handle it.

- Self banishing: playing music and banging pots/pans to scare it away, cleansing the air with incense or ethically sourced sage, putting out charged crystals, taking a shower or bath with sea salt and aromatherapy oils to aid the body in it's mental and physical recovery, thus fighting off the entity.

Spirits and shadow people

Have you ever caught a shadow out of the corner of your eye and felt a little uneasy? There hasn't been a definitive answer regarding shadow people but the consensus seems to be that these entities make us feel a bit on edge. They may not be malicious but it is terrifying having an opaque, featureless black entity appear in your home, which is something I have direct experience with. If you don't want to see them, tell the Universe. I say this especially at night if I ever feel uneasy.

Seeing spirit on the other hand is not a scary experience. Generally they look very well and ethereal. You might not see an entire spirit but a body part, such as hands, which I experienced one day. I was looking out the window, I was feeling tired and not thinking of anything in particular, when I looked down and saw a pair of hands cupping mine. They were the older hands of my relative and I felt such peace during this touching moment. There was no fear or stress, it was a really nice experience that I will remember fondly.

What is the difference between a ghost and a spirit?

Ghosts tend to be tied to their place of death or are unaware they have died. This can become problematic in such events where the house has been sold to new owners. The ghost doesn't understand who these people are and why they've taken over the house. To remove a ghost, making contact safely and explaining may work, or simply asking them to leave and cleansing the space should do the job.

Malicious entities can follow you, regardless of how many times you move house. Deal with the problem where you are first if possible. The added stress of moving home feeds it even more.

A spirit is a being who has passed over, has the freedom to travel the universe and lend a helping hand where possible. This spirit could be a grandmother who acts as a guardian angel, or your child who has passed away may surround you, bringing child-like joy and even moving your keys.

Mediumship

A psychic medium is a person who can make contact with those who have passed over and left their bodies behind. It takes a lot of time, effort and practice to hone this skill. It is also not wanted by everyone as it can bring some frightening or uneasy experiences particularly in childhood, cue the chorus of “I see dead people”.

Mediumship is generally done privately with their client, in a quiet space. They might hear what the spirit is saying, they may be shown images or memories which is why it can take some time to build up what spirit is saying. It can be difficult as well if there is a language barrier and the ancestor doesn’t speak the same language as the medium.

You can ask the spirit beforehand to come through for you and show a sign within reason, say to the psychic “I picked a number between 1 and 100, my loved one knows the number, can you confirm?” If you are feeling sceptical.

Ectoplasm is a material that forms during the channeling of spirit, and comes from the medium. A scottish medium, Helen Duncan was heavily involved in the research of ectoplasm. She passed away in 1956. During a seance in 1939, her ectoplasm was captured on photographic film and a sample was kept.

Ectoplasm is a material produced by the psychic as a by-product of channelling spirit and usually returns to the psychic, however it was captured in Ms Duncan's case. A French doctor in 1920 described his experiences with ectoplasm: “The color white is the most frequent.... On touch ... it can seem soft and a bit elastic when it spreads; hard, knotty or fibrous when it forms strings.... Sometimes it gives the sensation of a spider's web fluttering over the observers' hand.... The substance is mobile."

For ectoplasm to be witnessed, darkness is a must. It has some bio-luminescence, harsh lighting damages the ectoplasm.

It was once sought out heavily in science but became the butt of jokes, particularly when films such as ghostbusters came out and the ectoplasm was used for comedic effect.

Moon Rituals

"The sun sees your body. The moon sees your soul"
– [Ancient Proverb]

We touched on using the moon for manifestation and healing earlier in the book when working with menstrual cycles. The following is more detailed information on how to use the stages of the moon spiritually and or magically.

New Moon

A new moon is prime for setting intentions as it is the time for new beginnings. This is also a great time to clean the house and get prepared for this cycle to begin. Using some of last month's moon water, add a few drops of essential oils to your mop bucket for spiritually clean floors.

The new moon says "It's clearing out the old energy to welcome in those manifestations"! Write down the intentions and manifestations in a journal, you can even create a vision board.

First quarter

Use this energy to plan and prepare, get those manifestations and ideas off the ground. It's a great time to focus on the details. Continue to manifest, attract and be magnetic to the abundance of the universe. Try and stay on the frequency of abundance which you can listen to as you sleep, try - **183.58 Hz, 639Hz and 777 Hz.**

Full Moon

Celebrate and relax, the energies around full moons are very heavy and can bring on bouts of fatigue. Collectively, Ariana Palmieri calls it "a cosmic sigh."This year in 2021 there have been 4 supermoons in a row, and one of those supermoons landed in conjunction with an eclipse, an incredibly rare event indeed.

This is a good time to charge up crystals by placing them in the moonlight. You can also make moon water by placing water in a jar or a recycled bottle and place it to charge beside the crystals. Moon water can be used in spells, cleaning, banishing - it is multifunctional!

Many people get emotional or are quicker to react around full moons and some say "oh is there a full moon tonight?" in jest, not realising there is substance to this theory. As previously mentioned, the tide of our seas is controlled by the magnetic forces of our moon. Sea turtles and other animals rely on the moon for guidance, for example sea turtles use full moons as a guiding light back to the sea where their life cycle continues on.

If you tend to experience a menstrual period during this time, it's wise to avoid a heavy calendar in terms of work and social events where possible. It's best to rest up and enjoy some luxury goods such as chocolate or a face mask and show yourself some love.

A hot bath with epsom salts wouldn't go amiss, I sometimes use the remnants of last month's moon water to top up the tub with some good vibes.

Last quarter

The last quarter of the moon asks you to release what no longer serves you. Break it all down and see what building blocks you can take with you into the next lunar phase and stage of life. Doing a ritual such as a burning bowl is a great way to release things energetically and is physically cathartic when watching as the fire engulfs the paper.

Chapter Eight

If you believe in Astrology and Tarot as tools for divine information, then what are your thoughts on extraterrestrials? Is it so far-fetched to think another being in another galaxy might be doing something similar to try and work out what is happening in the universe?

Have you ever felt like an alien? Many people do. Many more believe they are souls here from another planet, living a human life to help the human race out. Which honestly isn't too far fetched for me considering the state of our planet. Mass murders, daily sexual assaults, genocides, war, famine, not to mention the day to day aggressions and stressors we experience, which push people to their limits. If there are souls here from far away, who want to help the dumpster fire that is humanity? I'm ok with that.

Let's get into the alien stuff! The following has been researched, referenced and fact checked.

There are many conspiracy theories involving aliens. There is also a fair whack of evidence to prove we are not alone but much of it is anecdotal, and the public wants something tangible before there is mass belief in aliens. However, there are structures on Earth that boggle most minds and therefore, are incredibly interesting to discuss here.

Firstly, let's look at the Great Pyramid of Giza in Egypt. This structure was approximately built between 2580–2560 BC and still stands to this day. The Great Pyramid is only a few degrees short of True North currently, but this is due to the earth's precession. If a line was drawn out from the centre of The Great Pyramid, there would be equal lines across the globe, making it a land mass centre, mathematically. The Great Pyramid was built 2000 years before Pythagorus created his theorem. This structure is more precise than many modern skyscrapers. The pyramid was first thought out by using a string with a weight on the end and they would line the string up with the stars.

There are more mathematical synchronicities such as:

- The building blocks of the pyramid units are in CUBITS, which is 1/25 million of the polar diameter of the earth, which is essentially perfection.
- Using the square base points, scientists found that it translates into 365.242 cubits, which is the same number as a tropical year on Earth.
- The Great Pyramid is in-line with the equator and acts as a scale model for the Northern Hemisphere.

- The coordinate of The Great Pyramid - 29.9792458°N is the same number sequence as the speed of light travelling through space in a vacuum.

Using string and the shadow of the day, the Ancients mapped out a replica of the build on the surrounding land. The build took around 14 years, with intense precision. Two blocks were laid approximately every 3 minutes and each block was around 2.5 tonnes. The Archeologist who identified the survey points for the build seems to think this build was an act of passion from the 25,000 men and not that of slaves. The pyramid is so precise, he seems to think it wouldn't have been constructed to a high standard if the enslaved people were forced to build.

Structures like the ones on Easter Island have often been thought to be alien made. However, the build of the Moai by it's Polynesian inhabitants seem to have built them to aid agriculture. For centuries scientists were baffled and tourists in awe by these huge structures, it is understandable to think they were made by aliens if you'd never seen anything like that before.

Stonehenge

The Stonehenge is another historical landmark in Salisbury, England and is a prehistoric monument dating as far back as 2000 BC. There have been recent findings in June 2021 that the stones were part of a neolithic temple. Druids have flocked to the site as a pilgrimage and historians have identified that it was a place of healing, rather than an attempt at a calendar.

Off Planet

NASA currently has the Perseverance rover on Mars collecting information on the geology of the planet and will have the first ever samples returned from Mars in 2031. An undergraduate at NASA identified water in the crater on Mars but this wasn't confirmed until 2015 steamrolling over the 1970s statement that Mars was a dry and barren planet.

Cassie Conley is the US planetary protection officer and works mainly with microorganisms to ensure that any coming or going will not affect life on other planets or here on Earth. In order to prove life on Mars, it cannot be contaminated in any way. White settlers brought smallpox to the Native American tribes, decimating them. This cannot be repeated.

When the first rover found water, it was her job to keep the rover away from the sample. In 1996, ALH84001 a Martian Meteor landed in Antartica which was consequently sampled and found to have bacterial chains similar to that on Earth - found in ponds - however, it was debated that this was in fact contamination.

Martians became a common name for aliens but there isn't any way to confirm what planet or star system an extraterrestrial comes from. The term Martian has been used in a plethora of science-fiction material such as cult classic - Mars Attacks! from Tim Burton.

Renowned astronomers, physicists and astrologers such as: Carl Sagan, Neil deGrasse Tyson and Vijayalakshmi Krishnan have wonderful information that is accessible. Dr Neil particularly has many amazing documentaries that have great visual examples.

"We are part of this universe; we are in this universe, but perhaps more important than both of those facts, is that the universe is in us" - Neil deGrasse Tyson.

"We're made of star stuff. We are a way for the cosmos to know itself" - Carl Sagan.

Carl Sagan's "Pale Blue Dot'" was an incredible insight into the insignificance of Earth and the significance of our actions on this Earth.

"The Earth is a very small stage in a vast cosmic arena. Think of the endless cruelties visited by the inhabitants of one corner of this pixel on the scarcely distinguishable inhabitants of some other corner, how frequent their misunderstandings, how eager they are to kill one another, how fervent their hatreds. Think of the rivers of blood spilled by all

those generals and emperors so that, in glory and triumph, they could become the momentary masters of a fraction of a dot. Our posturings, our imagined self-importance, the delusion that we have some privileged position in the Universe, are challenged by this point of pale light. Our planet is a lonely speck in the great enveloping cosmic dark. In our obscurity, in all this vastness, there is no hint that help will come from elsewhere to save us from ourselves.

The Earth is the only world known so far to harbor life. There is nowhere else, at least in the near future, to which our species could migrate. Visit, yes. Settle, not yet. Like it or not, for the moment the Earth is where we make our stand."

One of the most well known statements from Carl is "*the nitrogen in our DNA, the calcium in our teeth, the iron in our blood, the carbon in our apple pies were made in the interiors of collapsing stars. We are made of starstuff.*" Cosmos.

What a wonderful reminder of who we are and what we share with these colossal celestial beings in the sky, previously untouched and unknown by earlier humans.

There are vantage points in nearby star systems, such as the constellation of Virgo, where intelligent life would be able to view Earth from the dwarf planet (Ross 128). These systems are also close enough to receive 100 years worth of TV and Radio broadcasting, which is why it is so troubling; some of the first things aliens hear from us would be Nazi Propaganda. However, transmissions can be blocked by interfering stars, so we will have to wait and see.

There have been UFO sightings all over the world by people from a diverse range of backgrounds. Young to old people, different faiths, genders, skin colours, job, social status - and unfortunately, some people who are not believed become deeply troubled at the rejection from their fellow humans, ending up struggling with substance abuse or suicide because of the ridicule. It must be very difficult to have an experience that felt real, and was real to them, then have that discounted. We are living on a rock that is flying through space, what will be, will be. However, Murphy's law states: "Anything that can go wrong will go wrong", which is why NASA has such strict ways of dealing with space travel and any type of communication with extraterrestrials or "ETs".

Roswell

In the 1940's a 'UFO' crashed and was later revealed as a weather balloon which had been in testing to counter any Soviet technology, which had crashed on a farm in New Mexico. Project Mogul was eventually declassified, but as you can imagine there is much distrust and cover story upon cover story.

On the 15th of February 2021, the DIA (Defence Intelligence Agency) announced it had recovered UFO (Unidentified Flying Object) material, a metal named "nitinol" which has physical memory and can pop back when folded. Much of the report is redacted but there was mention of manipulating the speed of light by slowing it down and also compressising EMF energy (the very electromagnetic field discussed earlier).

One positive move by the President of the United States Donald Trump, requested that this information from the pentagon be released. He also admitted to being briefed at The White House regarding aliens. Recently, Donald Trump Jr. asked his father if he would ever disclose to the public about the alleged incident at Roswell in 1947, and his father said, "I won't talk to you about what I know about it, but it's very interesting." It did take a while but the information is accessible although much of it is redacted.

He seemed fairly calm and uninterested in the whole debacle, but it is wonderful that more information is becoming readily available. Many are worried there will be a future spilling of the beans by the former president, which is eagerly awaited by millions who have an interest in or have been affected by ETs.

In the 70s, Brad Steigner proposed in his book "Gods of Aquarius" that some, if not all humans, on Earth are aliens having a human experience. The new age theory was exponential during the 70s and I have to wonder if it's intrinsically linked to the psychedelic awakenings. Every drug should be used in moderation, and every tool can be used for good or evil things- it is in the hands of the person weaving it. Is it possible that during this decade, humans were so psychically open that they were able to communicate with their higher selves. There are also many theories that we are visited by other star systems.

Anecdotal evidence from abductions

Many people have experience with extraterrestrials and we are often obsessed with UFO documentaries as soon as the latest one comes out. There are series upon series of tv shows, from all over the globe where individuals discuss their alien experience.

Cinema goers were terrified by Mel Gibson's haunted character in "Signs"; a slow burner, psychological film about a farm that is being visited by aliens, directed by M. Night Shyamalan. However, it is not too distant from real life experiences.

In the United States of America in 1961, the first widely publicised alien abduction hit the newsstands. Betty and Barney Hill's abduction became known as the "Zeta Reticuli" incident due to the constellation their abductors had come from.

They were not harmed in any way, but have unexplainable memories and broken items from their time with extraterrestrials. Their clothing was disturbed, ripped and broken in places and both of their watches never worked again.

Whitley Strieber, a science fiction writer, was disturbed one evening in New York, where he was alone in a cabin in the woods. He observed a small non-human entity and then it was morning. He had another experience years later where he actually spoke to the being.

In 1978, Australian pilot Frederick Valentich disappeared after confirming over radio that he was being followed by an unidentified aircraft over the strait between Australia and Tasmania. He described the vehicle in detail, its movements and speeds, because the tower was not receiving any feedback from vehicles in the sky; to them it did not exist. "It's hovering and it's not an aircraft" were his last words. Frederick was never seen again, although there are visuals from witnesses to corroborate the story.

The experiences that people had are difficult to ignore. As science progresses, it is likely we will make discoveries that further prove there is other life in the galaxy. But until then, it is knowing deep down in your soul, that you are not from Earth.

Not of this planet

Starseeds are souls from other planets, mainly the Pleiades star system. They incarnate on this planet as a choice, to help humans and heal the Earth. Now, some may listen to this and think it is lunacy, but honestly, to assume we are the only "living" thing in the entire universe is arrogant and naive in my opinion. There are a billion-trillion stars in the universe, just to put a number on it!

Star seeds are said to have incarnated on Earth during the worship of Isis, a goddess with many powers.

"The cosmos are within us. We are made of star-stuff. We are a way for the universe to know itself." - Carl Sagan.

There are oracle decks for tarot readers that help identify what type of star seed you are, but it's really down to resonating with the information on a deep level.

How do I know if I am a star seed?

1. The word itself resonates with you, you may get shivers down your spine or enjoy saying it over and over.

2. You are drawn to the night sky and are fond of star gazing. You feel a sense of longing and wanting to go home.

3. You know there is more to life than the 9-5, but you are struggling to find purpose and feel hopeless and lost. (Many star seeds leave the capitalist system).

4. You struggle with authority and clash with police, government, teachers etc, not necessarily in an aggressive manner, but you want to go your own way.

5. You see synchronicities from the Universe and they resonate, you understand that you are being guided although you do not know where.

Different types of star seeds

Plaidean

Plaidean star seeds seem to be the most common, as there is the most research available about them. Constellations such as The Seven Sisters and Messier 45 make up the Plaideas. They are a matriarchal society which is possibly why so many are called to Earth, to work against the misogynistic society we live in.

Sirian

Sirian star seeds come from the Sirius A and B constellations of the Canis Major. According to evidence online, the awakening stemmed from Sirians and are the origins of ascended masters Jesus Christ and Mary Magdalene.

Arcuturian

Arcturian star seeds are the most advanced emotionally and said to be the blueprint for human life. Many shamans are Arcurian star seeds. Remember this is one of the brightest stars in the sky.

Andromedan

Andromedan star seeds are incredibly technologically advanced and are telepaths. They are from the Andromeda galaxy. They have energy in realms up to the 12th dimension. It is the nearest galaxy to Earth and is so bright it can sometimes be viewed from Earth.

Lesser known star seeds

Hadarian

Hadarian star seeds come from the Beta Centauri constellation which is a triple star system. There is a planet within this constellation named by humans as

"Hadar." A common physical trait amongst them is heterochromia - two different coloured eyes. They have a lot to give and often feel this isn't reciprocated on the level they desire. They will struggle with boundaries in relationships due to them seeking love. The goal of a Hadarian is how can they bring more love to the planet, and it is a difficult job to do in this climate.

https://www.spiritualunite.com/articles/hadarian-starseeds/

Now that the different types of star seeds have been covered, it is important to find like minded people, who are either empaths, highly sensitive or a star seed themselves. We do not come here alone.

Soul family

We often hear the term "soul mates" thrown around, but what are they? If you have actively done healing and trauma work, then the following should be safe information. If you have never been to therapy or identified toxic cycles within relationships, this can be difficult ground as narcissists can mimic some of these traits too. Soulmates inspire you to complete yourself; they teach you self-healing.

A soulmate is someone we feel at ease with. They are often labelled as romantic but this is not always the case. Soulmates can be sexual and romantic, but also familial in terms of chosen family and also platonic. Have you ever met someone you instantly vibe with? You meet and are able to have flowing conversation, establish emotional intimacy and even share a similar sense of humour. I believe there are soulmates for us at each new level of our lives. It is important to note that soul mates do not stay in our lives forever, but to be grateful for the time you do share. Sometimes, soulmates enter your life for a short time, but leave the most beautiful memories.

"When you meet someone new and your souls instantaneously recognise a piece of yourself deep within the other, and right away you both feel safe being your authentic self, that is a soul connection" - Carrie Love.

How to identify a soulmate connection:

- You feel at ease with this person
- A sense of familiarity or knowing you have met before
- Creation of a unique bond
- You can come home to this person, you can sit in silence together and just be
- You are two souls who find comfort in one another

What a romantic soulmate connection has to offer: intimate healing through mutual self love, a great match in terms of relationship values; they tend to be enlightening and help each partner heal from previous karmic relations. You are likely to have a lot in common and possibly similar childhoods in terms of being difficult.

Platonic soulmate connections offer: amazing friends, often ending up physically at a distance but the friendship continues. Time or space has no bearing on this connection and it always picks up where it left off.

Karmic partnerships

Karmic partnerships are usually very tumultuous and difficult relationships, typically in the form of romantic relationships but can also be friendships too. They are essential for spiritual growth because they trigger healing, although these relationships can be awful - fortunately, there is support out there for people in abusive relationships. Please don't be afraid to leave and start the healing.

The nature of a karmic partnership is to get the individual to understand the actions and behaviours that lie at the root of their karmic cycles. If a person doesn't heal childhood traumas, there is a very high chance they will have difficulties within interpersonal relationships.

Generally, karmic relationships bring about death and transformation of the soul as you shed what no longer serves you. The rewards from these relationships ending can often reveal themselves years later. These relationships are not built to last.

The goal with karmic relationships is to not have them anymore. You want to be healed to the point where you no longer attract people of a lower vibration. You only attract emotionally available people; individuals who will treat you respectfully and be loving with no strings attached.

Twin Flames

A twin flame connection is rare. It is the splitting of a soul into two bodies. These relationships are notoriously difficult in the beginning and can cause huge disruption in both partners' lives. Although union of twin flames is possible in this lifetime, it will take a lot of work from both parties to make it a viable relationship.

"Your Twin Flame is your perfect divine counterpart, created from Source from the same energy rays as you, thereby they are your mirror. They are you. You will feel this when you meet them" - Cassady Cayne.

Cassady Cayne is a degree educated psychologist and intuit, who began channeling twin flame messages throughout her own journey. Her website offers many free tools to help with the heavy energies that can consume twin flames. Her free pdf states:

"11:11 – Remembrance
Many of you experience a triggering event or period of time when you are spurred on to remember who you are as a soul. 11:11 is used as a trigger mechanism by your guides and angels to get your attention. Many numerical sequences maybe used for personal reference but 11:11 is a remembering of who you are, as well as a signal to pay attention and that we are by your side. The mirroring sequence of 11:11 specifically stands for a gateway, the two Twins unifying and bringing about a portal of source energy. The two parts become whole. If you are with someone and wondering if they are your Twin, this is a great indication from your guides that yes, they are.``

Many spiritual people are hidden in plain sight and the universe brings them to you for a specific reason. For example, when I was struggling with writer's block with this very book, I met a fellow dog parent who witnessed a bird flying around me. This is how the "signs from spirit" chapter came about! Some come by to relay a specific message unconsciously, and you may hear them say something in passing that resonates.

Twin flame madness hit social media platforms in 2021. There are many tarot readers that cater to twin flames and offer tarot turn flame readings.Twin flames are the same soul in two bodies and mirror each other. The levels of telepathy are off the scale and many even feel their twin flame's energies and physical sensations, which can be very disorientating when you're not able to distinguish if it's their energy or yours. Twins tend to dream about each other too. Twins can differ in age, commonly between 1- 20-ish years apart or so. Sometimes more. Having your partner be a mirror image of you tends to be triggering and quite upsetting, especially when you meet them and neither of you have started to do shadow work.

A twin flame runner and chaser dynamic can often show up as the anxious/avoidant attachment pattern. However, not everyone in this dynamic is a twin flame, which is why it is crucial to a) know the difference and b) go to therapy, do the shadow work, and focus on yourself, so that when someone does come along, you can identify of they are a karmic partner, a soulmate or a twin flame - which again, not everyone is a twin flame or has a twin flame. This is to do with "soul contracts" a belief in the spiritual community that souls who choose to come to Earth for a human life-time can also choose their level of difficulty in terms of: the family they incarnate into, their traumas, challenges to overcome, and this also can include romantic partners.

A soul can split into two bodies and thus the creation of a twin flame pair is created. Karmic partners are in our lives to teach us where we need to heal but this does not mean that anyone deserves to be mistreated or abused, in any way shape or form. Karmic relationships can be incredibly toxic but they do have the ability to transform a person, and it's up to them to transmute the trauma and the lessons into something new and positive, which is easier said and done. This healing can take a life-time.

The universe sends us lessons until we learn them; sometimes it feels like we keep dating people who are similar in their toxic traits and we must ask ourselves why this pattern continues. We can also experience toxic friends and this can be a really upsetting and disruptive time for an individual. These relationships can be prominent in a school environment, particularly during high school which are known for being breeding grounds for dramatic and often toxic situations.

Signs you have met your Twin Flame:

Intensity: intense eye contact, being able to read their face as easily as a book, feeling their intense energies in your physical body when separated or apart

Knowing: You know them. You are them. It is a very odd feeling and truly difficult to explain unless it has happened!

Rejection

Rejection is redirection; once I started to believe this affirmation, I realised I could take punches from the universe like a pro boxer. I realised I could pick myself up way quicker if I felt my feelings, then came up with a game plan. I would lie in bed for days, paralysed by fear and failure, unable to see through the fog of my disappointment. I never realised that it could be a gift, a blessing in disguise. I had such a negative mindset that I never thought to approach it in such a manner. The feelings are complicated and arguably the most challenging aspect. The job you didn't get, the person you desired didn't feel the same way, whatever it was, it was not for you, because something better is on its way to you. You must grieve. Then you must let the emotions leave like the visitors they are. Dodging a bullet doesn't mean you won't get scraped or hurt. Change can be pain-free, but it is a lesson that often takes a lifetime to master.

Let's look at romantic rejection.

When someone doesn't find us attractive, it can feel very personal. I remember feeling wounded and rejected by a prospective love interest and feeling that my appearance was not enough for them. This was, in fact, a deep-rooted insecurity which stemmed from childhood because I had to "look good" as I was a reflection of the family. When I wasn't looking up to standard, I would internalise it according to a family member. Then, as a young woman witnessing the misogyny of the beauty industry, the fatphobia, racism, colourism, homophobia, transphobia, it added fuel to the fire. So if someone didn't find me attractive, I would wonder what's wrong with me? Yet there was nothing wrong, it just means the other person has different tastes.

If we do not vibe with a person or find some aspect of their personality attractive, then it will be extremely unlikely that a relationship would form and stand the test of time. True matches in terms of energy are pretty rare, and you must be aware of how people make you feel. If you can't relax or sit in silence with this person, it's not a match. We all need downtime. If they make you feel drained or tired, do you want to be with this person?

Relationships should never be forced. The connection should feel easy and comfortable and the dynamic should feel safe.

The Universe protects us in mysterious ways. Here's an example: I've seen people get upset about not getting the job they wanted, then a few months later, the company goes bust, the universe knew you'd be back at square one again. There's a reason why some things just don't work out, which sometimes we see why almost immediately, and other times it does not become apparent for a long time. Sometimes never, until you have passed to the other side and can see the threads of time. Letting go is always difficult at first because we fear loss.

Conclusion

This audiobook has a variety of techniques and strategies to explore and it's easy to feel overwhelmed. Hopefully you feel inspired to try a few of these and integrate them into your practices. I would mostly like you to know that you are not alone in feeling strange or isolated. People want to be chosen but rarely realise it can be a lonely path if there is no one to guide you. Let this book be your guide and lead you to places and people that are good for you.

The key takeaways from this audiobook is cleansing and protection, as we empaths and highly sensitive people struggle immensely with other people's energies. Begin by doing these rituals and practices and the intuition will grow vastly. Put energy into yourself and boundaries and feel your energy levels rise immediately, it's shocking when you realise a friend is actually an energy vampire who you always felt ill around...

The divine practices will reveal themselves to you once you have improved your spiritual hygiene, clarity tends to come thick and fast as all your dominos fall into place. You can build the life you desire by learning the ways of the Earth and our solar system, using the law of attraction and your own magick to bring about the changes you've fantasised about since childhood. It's not a joke or some pyramid scheme gimmick, there are invisible tools available to us and it is time to wake up and use them. Step into your power, your wisdom and your knowledge that has been passed down by your ancestors. This is accessible to you if you tap into your inner magick.

There are some shadow work journal prompts followed by guided meditations, both of which are incredibly healing. Trauma, feelings and emotions must be brought to the surface in order to be felt and processed and there are many ways to do this.

Please be kind to yourself as you work through these techniques as it can be very emotionally taxing. I saw a wonderful quote the other day that said "when you think everyone hates you, go to sleep. When you think you hate everyone, you need to eat" and I thought that was pretty spot on advice. Eat well as much as you can, sleep when you can and be kind to everyone, especially yourself. There is only one you.

Shadow Work and Journal Prompts

Please seek help, therapy or support where possible if you begin to feel triggered and overwhelmed by the following. Shadow work is incredibly difficult and should be approached when you are feeling well, in order to have a balanced perspective on what is surfacing. This shadow work can be used to help with repressed aspects of the personality that was likely squashed in your formative years.

What belief has been ingrained in me since childhood?
[pause]

When this belief was challenged how did I react?

[pause]
Who or what taught me these beliefs?

[pause]

Repeat this affirmation either internally or out loud:

"Now, when I am given new information I can think critically and come to my own conclusions."

"I love my shadow, they are a part of me that had a specific job to do, and for that I am so grateful."

"I love the parts of myself that helped me survive. I have much to unlearn and must be kind to myself, including my shadow."

The second part of this shadow work asks you to take a look inside with a magnifying glass. Again, use the journal prompts with care and please seek support as required.

What part of myself scares me the most?

[pause]

Why?

[pause]

When was this part needed? Or when did this part take over?

[pause]
What soothes this part of yourself?

[pause]

Can you self-soothe as a whole?

[pause]

Congratulations, this therapy technique called internal family systems has helped you in your shadow work session today. This is a renowned technique used by therapists across the globe to help identify fragmented parts of self that broke off possibly after a traumatic event. We often find that parts stay the same age as when the event happened. You are essentially re-parenting yourself by using positive internal thoughts and managing your inner child with the love and compassion you deserved as a child.

Ifs is a great tool for people who are integrating parts and also for those with did, dissociative identity disorder. Some people have systems and are aware of the other personalities, they can share information and memories. It does not mean you are crazy, many people hear voices in a non psychotic manner.

Guided Meditations

Pace: Slow and sincere, our readers/listeners want to be soothed and need to be calm for the rest to align with them. It takes beginners longer to settle and they need a lot of awareness to help them experience their body somatically. Then we need to create a calm space and discuss intrusive thoughts and how to acknowledge them and let them go. Explaining mindfulness is not having an empty mind but identifying when you are thinking heavily on a particular topic that doesn't serve you either in that moment or this is presented as a fact.

Guided Meditation One

Welcome to your guided meditation, my name is ______. This journey will take you upstream to a hidden cavern that only you know. Together, we will work on some aspects of the psyche, and you will return feeling reinvigorated with a new perspective. Guided meditations should not be listened to when driving or operating machinery. Please allow yourself to get comfortable, whether that's sitting down or lying down with a blanket. Close your eyes and let's begin.

Start by taking a deep breath in. Taking the breath in through the nose, allowing the abdomen to stretch all the way out, and releasing the breath by exhaling through the mouth. Notice how deep the breath is, all the way into the abdomen, slowly taking up space. Keep breathing deeply, inhaling through the nose and out through the mouth. Allow your shoulders to relax. Are they moving when you inhale?

Allow each shoulder to drop. Each inhale should be led by the diaphragm and the shoulders follow suit. This can be a different way of breathing for some, keep trying! You are doing a great job. If you feel your shoulders tensing again, bring back awareness to your breathing. It is all about the repetition.

Through each breath we get more and more aware of the body. Now we are calming down, to a state of mindfulness, are there any areas in the body that feel tense or stressed?

Take this opportunity to wiggle your fingers and toes. Roll your neck from shoulder to shoulder, slowly, savouring the stretch from side to side. Open your jaw for a big, long yawn. Allow yourself to relax.

Repeat this affirmation either internally or aloud:

"I allow myself to relax. I release myself of the stress and burdens I carry. I allow my deep breaths to bring in mindfulness and awareness of this incredible body. I am taking this time for myself, it is essential for my health."

Let us board the vessel and head up stream. The beautiful calm waters are a sparkling blue, reflecting a clear sky. Feel the heat in the air, as the sun rises on another incredible day. Moving slowly and steadily up the river, you can hear the water gently lapping the sides. Birds sing in the distance, bees buzzing along the banks, saying hello to the wild flowers.

We travel further from humanity and further into nature. We no longer hear the hustle and bustle of the city but pure, natural sounds from the Earth. You realise this, as you take in another deep, satisfying breath through your nose and slowly exhaling out.

Notice that you cannot hear any vehicle on the land or in the air, no machine noises to crowd the airwaves. Only the sounds that our ancestors heard, the sounds of our world.

The sun on your face feels pleasant, and you see the orange glow through your eyelids. Let the energy of the sun power you up, like a plant, he feeds us too. Allow the sunlight to clear your energy field, reset your body and remove all blocks that you are currently experiencing.

The river heads towards the open sea, but there is a small passage leading into a gorgeous rock formation standing in the distance. Taking the smaller stream, the vessel goes gently towards the cave.
The entrance is a large, smooth entryway, covered in lush greenery. There is deep green seaweed embellished with shells, reflecting the sun, who shines in through the opening at the top of the cave. The vessel comes to a stop. Climbing out, feeling the wet sand below and the cool sea water, you can see how clear the water is. A faint rush of water can be heard, and over to the left of the cave is a small waterfall surrounded by a clear body of water. You close your eyes and melt into your surroundings.

Let us sit in this beautiful place. Breathe deeply and take in the sounds of the gentle waterfall, and hear the water lap at your feet. Notice the silence of humanity and embrace the sounds of nature. Allow the energy from this ancient cave to remind you, that you too are an old soul who has healed many times before. You have stood against the tests that have arisen over time, and unmoving, unwavering like stone, you are still here. For that I am grateful.

Place a hand on your heart and a hand on the abdomen. Inhale deeply, and repeat this affirmation internally or verbally:

"I am safe and protected here. It is me and my guide, surrounded by nature and deep gratitude. This is a calm place where I can focus on my healing. This beautiful cave lets the light in, and I allow the light to cast a shadow, so that they may come back to the self, and we can be one again. I am safe and protected here."

In this beautiful, sacred place, we will work on some core beliefs. Please allow the tears to flow if they come, as it is a wonderful way to express yourself. Remember, you are safe and protected here. Notice any thoughts that come up. Acknowledge those thoughts, then let them float away. Sometimes they appear strong and sudden, but pass eventually like a ripple in the water. Thoughts and feelings come and go, they do not define us.

Repeat these affirmations **either internally or aloud**:

"I am enough. I am good enough."

"I am not too much or too little. I am perfect in my imperfect way."

"Each day I strive to be better than I was yesterday."

"I am a good person."

"I have love to give and I am open to love."

The sun shines in through the opening and its brightness envelops you. A white light begins to move in waves, shining through your entire being. Let it reach the parts of you that are hidden away. Let the light reach the parts that are hurting and experiencing trauma. This glorious white light resonates through you, each wave more healing than the last.

The Universe sees you. She loves you. She knows you have been through some shit. This is your chance to offer it up and let it go. Let the tears flow and the sobs out or grin the biggest grin, it is human to emote. Release all the negativity, let it all go.

Imagine how good it feels, when the water washes away the dirt off your skin after a long day in the garden, watching the dirt leave your body and exit down the plughole of the shower is satisfying - allow your energy field to do the same. Imagine the negative energy as dirt being washed away, leaving never to be seen again. Soon we will enter this calm, clear pool.

Release all that no longer serves you. Drop the perceptions and expectations of society. They are not you. Release the pressure from your nearest and dearest, let the projections go. You are you and not what they expect you to be.

Release the comparisons; they thieve your joy. That person on social media does not have it all, because many have not yet woken up to the fact, everything we need is inside of us. Experiences are what open us up, and we learn more skills. You keep levelling up, it is so inspirational to see. I am so proud of you!

Look at you taking time for yourself, uninterrupted. I love this form of self-care for you. I can feel how relaxed you are! Look how deeply you are breathing! This is how to access the parts of yourself that need recognition or some TLC. I love that you understand that nurturing yourself first means you can nurture others. No-one can pour from an empty cup.

Think about the best version of yourself. What are they like? What morals and values do they have? Take a moment to think about this, hold the question in your mind's eye. Let your intuition speak, you are wonderfully relaxed and in tune with yourself.

[pause]

Now you know what your future self stands for, think for a moment how you can bridge the gap between you and them. This can be something seemingly

small and insignificant, like getting up at 7am each day without fail. Can you add in this small thing? Can you make it a healthy habit? Yes!
What things are you still holding on to? Thank them for the lessons and let them go. Whether it's friends, family, intimate relationships or a horrible job, life is too short for things that make you unhappy.

Repeat these affirmations **either internally or aloud**:

"I release all negativity from my life. I cut all cords with those who bring me harm and the energy will be RTS, return to sender."

"I release the old and welcome the new. I am grateful for my blessings and thankful for those lessons".

Now it is time to meet the part of yourself that you keep hidden away. They are so in need of your love. Your shadow is the subconscious part of you, your memories, traumas, projections, judgements. All the things society says cannot be, yet it is. The shadow exists in us all, and is not inherently bad. Everything we have internalised is held in our shadow. What a burden that must be to carry, shall we not help them? Without the shadow of the day we cannot tell the time. Without the night we cannot rest. They need us and we need them.

Repeat these affirmations **either internally or aloud**:

"I love my shadow and I love myself entirely."

"I love my shadow and I love myself entirely."

"I love my shadow and I love myself entirely."

"Each day I choose to be a better person."

"My shadow holds the lessons that taught me the most"

Dip into the water. It is as warm as a bath and only as high as your waist. The water is crystal clear and quiet, except for the ripples from the waterfall. It is time for you both to become one under the healing waterfall.

Allow the waterfall to cleanse your soul. Let it take away all your stresses and worries. Understand that you did the absolute best that you could, during the hardest times of your life. We can only use the tools available at the time. You have nothing to feel guilty or ashamed about.

Repeat this affirmation **either internally or aloud**:

"Shame is not mine to carry, I let it go."

"I was only a child. I did not deserve to be treated like that or experience those things."

"I am proud of myself and how far I have come."

"My self worth is not based on how others view me."

Imagine the light and dark becoming one. See the Yin and Yang, the duality, the balance that is so needed. This is you now. You are balanced and calm. You breathe deeply now, nourishing all of you with deep, loving breaths. You release what no longer serves you with ease. You flow like water, you are a serene being.

Let the water wash over you. It is so wonderfully warm. This beautiful salt water cleans out your wounds, adds texture to your hair. It feels as though the sun has been locked into your skin, and will be with you always.

You feel lighter, brighter, happy and grateful. The weight has been lifted off your shoulders. Your burdens are being released. The white healing light and healing waterfall combined have left you reinvigorated and rejuvenated. Your cup is full. You are so capable of anything you set your mind to.

You walk back to the vessel with a spring in your step, and an incredible smile upon your face. Your eyes show happiness and contentment, and this healing cave has done its job. This place is always inside you, you know how to get here. It is always safe and protected. You can come here anytime you like.

Repeat this affirmation **either internally or aloud**:

"I thank this healing space. I am grateful. I know this place is in my heart and can be accessed any time I desire."

The vessel gently moves back towards the cave entrance. Take this opportunity to breathe deeply. Inhale deeply through your nose, deep into your abdomen and hold the breath for five seconds. Exhale through your mouth for seven seconds. Repeat this twice.

[pause]

Upon leaving the cave, you can tell it has been a glorious day, as we emerge on a hot summer's evening. You are met with a glorious orange sunset, which looks like it takes up the whole sky. Pinks merge into oranges, the light blue sky starts to turn navy if you look far enough. Some stars are beginning to appear, and twinkle at you proudly. Did you know you are made of the same stuff that stars are made of?

That's right, you are a celestial being.

You lie back on the vessel, slowly moving downstream and begin to spot shooting stars. What are you wishing for?

You are worthy of your dreams. Your goals and ambitions are valid. You have everything you need within yourself. True success is experiencing happiness daily.
As we trundle along the river, think of times where you felt joy. Reflect on how you felt in that moment. Were any of those things related to childhood? What activities did you do as a child? Is there anything you've always wanted to try? What can you do to make your inner child happy?

[Long pause]

Your inner child is you, before society got its hands on you and twisted your perception of self. They deserve to be honoured and expressed. It's ok to act silly, or put on costumes. Some people bake, some paint. Some people found a sport in childhood but whatever it is, do your thing. Allowing your inner child's needs to be met is an incredibly healing experience. And here you are putting the work in! I am so proud of you.

Can you tell yourself that every day? Speak to yourself as though you were talking to a dear friend. I bet you wouldn't say half the stuff to them you say to yourself. You are being kind and compassionate to yourself, that is true strength.

The river laps quietly and the cicadas chitter. It is a warm evening and all the stars are out now. We slowly head back from the healing space to rejoin humanity with a new perspective. You feel lighter and brighter, you are on a journey of self love.

Take a deep breath in and wiggle your toes, as we start to bring awareness back to your body. Begin to roll your ankles on the exhale. Do the same for your fingers and stretch out on the exhale. Feel how calm and relaxed your body is. This is the baseline we must always return to. I am so glad you are feeling good! Our vessel finally stops and allows you to disembark. What a beautiful journey of self-love.

Remember, there is no rush. Remain where you are and continue with some breath work, someone might need a cup of tea or will get up and dance. Whatever you do after this guided meditation, do it with self love.

Love and light to all of you. I have been your guide ________, and I look forward to working with you again.

Guided Meditation Two - opening up to intuition

Welcome to your guided meditation, my name is ______. This journey will take you to a beautiful meadow, where together we will work to open you up spiritually, in a space where you are protected and loved. Please allow yourself to get comfortable, whether that's sitting down or lying down with a blanket. Close your eyes and let's begin.

We are walking to a beautiful meadow, on this summer evening, to spend the Solstice with the stars. What an incredible evening to open yourself up to the universe and be welcomed. Gaia is in full bloom, showing us what can be achieved when we rest, recuperate and listen to our intuition.

We cannot flower and bloom 365 days of the year. Like the moon, we must ebb and flow, stand confidently then rest, feel our emotions and express them. This meadow is hallowed ground. It is sacred and special, protected and connected to the stars. Nothing and no one can harm you here.

As we near the meadow, you can hear the crackles of the fire calling you to come and sit down. Feel the warmth and let it envelop you. With a blanket on your shoulders and the crackling fire, you are content. Looking up at the sky you can see the stars. There's no light pollution here, you can see it all. You can see a Nebula with the naked eye, gorgeous swirls of blue and purple, with twinkles coming from within it. You are looking at the same sky your ancestors gazed at. Whenever you feel alone, know that everything you need is inside you, including them.

Grounding and feeling the body becomes the focus now.You slowly return to Earth, and begin to ground yourself by taking a deep, deep breath in through your nose. Let this breath reach all the corners of your being. This deep breath is so satisfying. Exhale through your mouth, allowing your shoulders to drop. The crackles bring back your awareness, along with another deep breath in and out.

Let your body relax and sink into your surroundings. Feel your body be supported by the structure upon where you sit, or lie. You feel no pain, only awareness of areas that are starting to relax. Begin to loosen the jaw. Close your eyes and stretch it out, take your tongue off the roof of your mouth for a moment. Roll your neck, starting with your chin to your chest, then slowly taking it to the right shoulder. Inhale deeply in this position, and on the exhale move back to the centre. Inhale, and roll your neck to the left shoulder, exhaling as you hold this light stretch. Inhale and return to centre, exhaling through your mouth.

Placing a hand on your heart and the other on your abdomen, feel yourself at peace. Notice how calm your heart beat is. Your stomach is calm and steady. This is your natural state, your baseline.

Bring awareness to your hips and glutes. Are you holding stress in these areas? Relax the hamstring and glute muscles, you are safe and protected here. Feel your back relax as you release these areas that have been wound tightly for too long.

Now that your body has totally relaxed, release the areas that held your stress, notice how much better you feel already. The big secret to intuition is self-care and rest. Learning to love yourself and getting to know yourself in a calm state is sometimes a foreign concept, but here you are, putting the work in. Intuition, creativity, clarity – all of these things tend to appear when we are focused and relaxed. The two coexist rather well. Let us bring the focus to your healing now.

A white healing light, with a blue centre appears from the fire. Floating over slowly, and softly resting down on you like a veil. Let this pure, healing light in. Allow it to cleanse away all negative energies. Allow the light to shine on the parts of you that need a little more love today. Let this light surround you and become part of your aura, always healing and protecting. The veil transforms into pure light as you both become one.

Take a few moments to imagine this healing light moving through your body. Moving through the

bloodstream and reaching each cell. Firing through each and every neuron in the brain, cleansing and healing you from inside out. This light promotes healing and cell regeneration, you no longer feel exhausted. Mentally, you feel as though the cobwebs have been cleared. You feel lighter and brighter, and are now ready to approach your psychic awakening on this beautiful evening, witnessed by the stars.
Focusing on the dancing flames of the fire, imagine this deep red colour as a ball of energy. This deep, intense red represents our root chakra which is located at the base of the spine. Hold this ball of energy in between your hands. Thank it for the stability and security it brings, and place the ball of energy at the base of your spine.

Next, within your hands an orange ball appears, representing the Sacral chakra. This chakra encourages you to accept your sexuality and understand that you have the ability to create. Thank it, and place it under the belly button.

A glowing yellow, bright as a daffodil appears in the palm of your hands, and asks you to step into your confidence. The Solar Plexus chakra is now balanced, and you will be able to discern gut instinct and intuition. Place this ball at your diaphragm.

The Heart chakra, as green as the meadow, blooms with love and empathy for the self, and others. Hold this ball of energy in your heart. Let the green light waves roll through your body, allowing yourself to crack open and be vulnerable to love. There is nothing to fear, the universe has your back.

A light blue energy ball appears, feel this in your hands and hold them over your throat. The throat chakra asks you to stand up for yourself and others, using your voice to educate and show compassion. Take no shit but do no harm, it says. Thank it and welcome this power into your body.

The third eye chakra, just above the physical eyes, is a beautiful indigo colour. Focus on this for a moment, imagining a third eye on your forehead, opening up for the first time and blinking. You have three eyes now. Two to look and one to see. Let this indigo energy bring in the knowledge of the universe, allow your perceptions to be changed by your inner knowing. This confidence you gained earlier is crucial for this journey. You should be so proud of yourself.

Finally, the Crown chakra, represented by a stunning white and violet light connects you to spirit and the universe, like an antenna. You are balanced, detached, in love with life. You are now truly open to the guidance of the universe.

You have now opened the seven major chakras, and have this information for the rest of your life, I admire your ability and eagerness to learn.

Repeat these affirmations **either internally or aloud**:

"I am divinely guided and supported by the cosmos."

"I have opened myself up to divine guidance."

"I have psychic gifts and abilities, awakening."

"I trust my body."

"I trust my gut."

"I am learning how my intuition speaks to me."

We are now moving into a moment of solitude. I am now guiding you deeper and deeper into yourself. Let your entire being relax. You are covered by the blanket of the universe, and now we count down.

Ten

Slowly, relaxing and surrendering to the infinite wisdom of the universe

Nine

Accepting that surrender is a necessary part of life

Eight

Balance is forming for you right now

Seven

Your luck will never run out. You make your own luck

Six

Feeling the healing hands of the universe

Five

Total relaxation washes over you

Four

Deeper and deeper

Three

You are connected and protected here

Two

Deeply calm and relaxed

One

You are in a deeply zen state

[five minute instrumental, healing frequency 852]

Like the moon, each of us has a dark side. This is not something to fear, but rather another part of you to love. The dark side of the moon represents intuition, knowing, secrets and mysteries. Allow this part of yourself to step forward. The magician or the high priestess, whoever you identify with. You are a magical being and have the power to see beyond the physical realm. You control what comes to you, in what method and what you tolerate.

Choose to only move with love and light. Lower vibrational beings are actively repelled by your light, nothing can touch you. Your light emanates over space and time. Call upon your angels, soul family, animals who are on the other side – only those who have the purest intentions towards you can enter your space. We all love you so much! Do you know that? You are so, so loved.

Now that your third eye is open, you will begin to seek more knowledge. You are going to see so many synchronicities that just cannot be ignored. Things are about to be so uncanny, you can't make it up. Trust and believe in divine guidance, and laugh or cry when needed.

Numbers, repeating numbers, on social media, car registration plates, analogue clocks, page numbers, receipts. They will be there. Synchronicities are signs of guidance and support.

Did you know you can ask the universe for signs? Specific signs? It can be in the form of car alarms going off, or seeing a big ginger cat! Make it personal to you and they become easier to spot.

After this guided meditation, observe how many feathers you spot. When you check your phone is it 11:11? Are you seeing more wild animals? Rabbits, birds, cats? Do dogs come over to say hi?

Soon you will start to notice things. You know what people are going to say. You can clock someone's energy the minute they enter a room. You hear your intuition. You hear the voices of your past selves cheering you on. This voice speaks up when you've seen something before, and tells you to avoid it to prevent another sore lesson. Your intuition is becoming an innate part of you that is wide awake and fully at your disposal. You know when someone is sending ill intent at you. Return to sender. This cannot even touch you.

In order to maintain these gifts that you have been given. You are asked to hold compassion and empathy for yourself and others. You are called upon to help other people, whether you use magick or the mundane, this life is all about human connection and helping others. Do not seek revenge. Know that the Universe has it all handled. Keep your head high and carry on.

You are asked to listen to the younger generations. Intelligence does not always increase with age, and children are the most psychically open beings on the planet until society deems it wrong. Encourage the upcoming generations. Show them love for their authenticity! You are stepping into your leadership role. You are becoming wise and knowing. Look around and take in the view.

You are a psychic being. You have the power to see. You have the power to discern. You can see auras. You can manipulate energy. The only limits are the ones you place upon yourself.

You are feeling strong, and powerful. You are awake to the infinite possibilities and feel pure gratitude for this journey. In your day to day life you are now noticing the magickal things the universe has for us on Earth.

The fire crackles again, slowly bringing your awareness back to the meadow. It was once a roaring fire and is now calming down to a small flame. The crackles and pops are soothing and satisfying.
Take a deep breath in through your nose. Hold the breath in the chest cavity and stretch your lower abdomen out, then exhale through your mouth. Let it all go. The Universe has your back and your gifts have been awakened. It is now time to close down.

You can do the following actions in your mind, or physically. Whichever you prefer.

From your crown chakra, take off your crown and place it in the fire.

Touch your third eye with your forefinger, and then point to the fire, returning the energy from this chakra.

Blow the fire with a kiss from your mouth using your hand. The throat chakra is now at baseline. Sing and speak your truth to channel this energy.

Hold your hand over your heart for 5, 4, 3 , 2 , 1 and move your arm out slowly, as if opening a door. If you love then let it go, what is ours will always return to us.

Rubbing your abdomen in a clockwise motion, allowing the energies from the solar plexus to move once more around the body.

Place thumb to thumb and forefinger to forefinger to create a triangle. Place this at pubic bone and hold for 3, 2, 1, thanking the Sacral chakra.

Finally, the Root chakra. Imagine a strong tree, a Redwood, standing strong for all eternity. Give the tree a hug. This is your tree, and it will always be there.

It is essential to open and close psychically to maximise and protect your gifts.

What a wonderful evening, we have learned so much. The fire is dying out now and it is time to go to bed. A comfortable hammock awaits you, adorned with sheepskin to keep you warm overnight, as you share the crisp evening with the stars.

You smile a big smile, because tonight you have awakened your gifts.

And now you will sleep, so deeply.

You are protected in the realms of your dreams by the highest power. You are protected in the 3D realm, physically by the highest power. Whatever you believe, hold your belief in your mind's eye. You live your life as a good person. You take the time for your personal growth. You try to understand others with compassion and empathy. For this you will always be rewarded with the best intentions and guidance.

Your body is healing and regenerating during sleep. During your sleep the white healing light continues to work its magic on your physical being. Tomorrow you will wake up feeling so well. You will wake up feeling refreshed. You can see a noticeable difference in your face, your eyes are sparkling and skin feels plump. You feel as though you are being pulled, taught by a string, walking or sitting tall. You can achieve anything today, invigorated by the powers of the Universe.

Notice what signs come up for you this day.

You are enough. You are grateful. You are loved.

As we come to the end of this guided meditation, I ask you to bring awareness to your breath, and allow it to fill up your body with active energy. You feel so refreshed and rejuvenated, full of yourself in the best way. Be kind and gentle with yourself for the hour following this guided meditation. Please consume a glass of water, and a small snack if you are hungry. Thank you for being here today and taking this time for yourself. It is an act of bravery in this world.

Thank you for listening to this guided meditation, I _____, have been your guide. Let me take a moment to congratulate you, and thank you for going on this journey, to find your inner gifts. This meadow is sacred, and will always be here for you. I will be here to meet you, any-time. Good-bye for now dear friend, and have a wonderful sleep.

Guided Meditation Three - manifesting abundance and practising detachment

Welcome to your guided meditation, my name is ______. This journey will take you to a fabulous Manor, where you will learn to manifest, in a space where you are protected and loved. Please allow yourself to get comfortable, whether that's sitting down or lying down with a blanket. Close your eyes and let's begin.

You are pulling up to a magnificent manor, that was hidden by the forest and couldn't be seen from the main road. The tyres move slowly, crunching over the gravel stopping at the main entrance. Looking through the car window, you can see the manor is made from light sandstone. Two pillars either side of the entrance are entwined with blooming jasmine, and the smell is divine.

You step out and experience the grandeur. Turning away from the manor, the garden beckons and is in full bloom. You can hear the bees buzzing, delighted to be out and about now that the pressure has lifted and the rain has gone. You take a moment to head over to the garden and take it all in.

There are sections to the garden and you can tell the flowers have been carefully selected and planted. The roses are full and aromatic; bright yellow ones and ruby red roses growing side by side. Peonies follow the roses, and their thick petals are a light pink. Walking around the garden you meet the tall sunflowers, who are easily 5 feet tall already.

Following on from this, there is a little herb garden, and you can smell the rosemary , thyme and wild garlic. The herbs are accompanied by tomato and capsicum plants, creating hot, spicy peppers and juicy tomatoes. Turning to head back the way, you see a lovely bright blue Emperor butterfly, settling on one of the sunflowers, basking up the warmth of the sun, drying its wings after being caught in the rain.

Hearing the crackle of the gravel brings you back to the awareness that it is time to enter the manor.
Heading indoors, you see the interior is white and decorated with artwork, marble sculptures and lush green plants. The floor is marble and your footsteps reverb as you walk slowly, taking in this beautiful environment.

You continue further into the manor and hear running water. You look to your right, peaking into a large room where there is an indoor water feature, trickling. Koi fish swim through their indoor pond, where they are loved and cared for.

Walking further into this massive place, a door on your left piques your interest. Inside is a vast library, with all the classics available. There is the cosiest looking armchair positioned near a lit fireplace, what a wonderful place to get lost in a book.

Upon leaving the library you notice the immaculate open plan kitchen and catch the scent of freshly baked bread and pastries. The smell is hypnotising as you wander over. The kitchen view is that of the garden, with huge patio doors ready to swing open when it's time to gather ingredients from the garden.

This place feels expensive, yet there are no brand names. It feels full of wisdom and knowledge. This manor feels like the success of someone's hard work coming to fruition. You are here because you are about to learn how to make this a reality for yourself.

Slowly walking out of the kitchen, you see the hallway further down reach a set of stairs. You take your time, absorbing in how bright this place is and how lush the house plants are. You reach the very top of the staircase and see down below, there are three doors equally spaced apart. This lesson in abundance has begun. With each step down towards the doors you will become infinitely more relaxed and aligned with the universe.

There are 10 steps, and you place your hand on the marble bannister as you make your way down.

Ten, releasing any negative energies from your being

Nine, beginning to feel more calm and relaxed

Eight, feeling deeply calm and content

Seven, knowing that you make your own luck settles your being even more

Six, your body is feeling so light and relaxed

Five, you are noticing how mindful your head-space feels as you slip deeper and deeper into relaxation

Four, self-care is necessary to create abundance and you are feeling content within

Three, almost at the bottom, a sense of joy washes over you

Two, feeling deeply relaxed

One, you feel confident and calm as you step on to the marble floor and meet the three doors.

Above the first door is a plaque that says “money manifestation.” You go to knock on the door, but it opens for you, and you enter.

Inside is a room, this room has every outfit you have ever longed for. Put something on that you feel good in! How does this outfit make you feel? Do you feel powerful? Seen? Validated? How would you dress now that money is not in short supply?

With a click of your fingers you are transported to a gorgeous hotel, very bourgeois. The bed is a super king size and is covered in luxurious fabrics. You walk over to the window, where are we? Take in this incredible view

[pause]

All of this can be yours in reality. It is yours in reality because your frequency matches that of abundance. Money is money whether it is £2 or 2 million pounds. You attract financial abundance regardless of the amounts. You understand that receiving this abundance is about sharing the wealth with others and seeing their joy and relief. Supporting people whilst unplugging them from the matrix and creating a space for undertaking change in their mental reprogramming, is truly a gift.

You are able to support causes you care about. You are able to buy anything you require at any time.

Repeat these money affirmations after me **either internally or aloud**:

"Money flows to me like water."

"I am abundant."

"I am financially wealthy and healthy."

"I share my wealth with others and for the good of humanity."

"Money and I vibrate at the same frequency."

Money in the form of paper notes begin to fly in, more and more notes pile up around you. Your wealth is now generational and you are creating an infinite resource pool. With this knowledge, you exit through the door you came in, with money stashed in your new outfit.

Upon stepping out, you feel a breeze of fresh air and take the opportunity to inhale deeply. Breathing in through your nose and out through your mouth, and again in through your nose. Holding the breath for 3, 2, 1 and out through the mouth.

Let us see what the second door holds for you.

It opens up and you shield your eyes from a beautiful bright light, which calms to a soft pink colour. Inside is a Greek palace. Marble sculptures of Aphrodite adorn the room, there are five each in a different pose. There is a plaque at the bottom of each sculpture.

The first sculpture has Aphrodite pouring an amphora, with water leaving out perfectly sculpted. The plaque states "ACTS OF SERVICE ". This is when you do something to relieve a burden or aid a loved one by performing an act.

The second sculpture has Aphrodite holding a glass hourglass. The plaque says "QUALITY TIME". This love language asks for devoted and uninterrupted time together with a loved one.

Third, Aphrodite mid speech – hand raised and palm up, draped in a wonderful toga. "WORDS OF AFFIRMATION" gives reassurance through words. A kind word goes a long way.

In this sculpture, Aphrodite embraces herself in a hug, holding herself tightly. The plaque reads "PHYSICAL TOUCH", a love language to create intimacy through non sexual touch.

Aphrodite is sculpted with her arms open, ready to receive.

"RECEIVING GIFTS" is the final love language, whereby they enjoy being thought of, and gifted by their loved one. This does not have to be expensive or materialistic whatsoever.

How do you show others love? Does this match the way you want to be loved? Are you open to receiving love as well as giving? Take a moment to think about how you currently receive love, and how you WANT to receive love.

[Pause – 4 minutes]

Repeat these affirmations **either internally or aloud**:

"I am loved."

"I am open to love"

"My heart chakra is open."

"I am learning about my love languages."

"I love myself wholly and fully, I forgive myself for my past mistakes."

"I love my physical body."

"I am proud of my body."

"I am so in love with myself and my life."

You feel moved by the goddess and are so grateful for these lessons in love. Your heart has been cracked open for the better. You now attract friends and partners who are full of love and able to receive love. You are emotionally available, as are your new friends.

A huge wave of self love washes over you, as you leave this room behind.

Once again, you feel the soft, light breeze against your skin and you take this opportunity to take a deep, deep breath in through your nose. Holding the breath for 3 seconds, 3, 2 , 1 and releasing the breath on the exhale.

Door 3 – healing

You move towards the door, when it opens you see a gorgeous healing space that has white light seeping in through the leaves of all the trees up high. You are in a forest and were invited by the Celtic people for a sacred healing ceremony. You walk along the forest floor that is covered in leaves, you hear your feet crunch against them. It is so quiet and calm here.

Welcome to this wonderful environment where you will be called to manifest your own healing in a safe sacred space.

After walking you finally reach a clearing, which opens up into a Glen. You can see the rolling hills for miles and feel your feet sink into the soft mossy grass. Many healers have been here before and you are another healer in a long line and there will be many after you, you are not alone.

In this clearing there are rocks with moss that are comfortable to sit on, you take a seat whilst the druid starts the fire. You are so welcome here, we are so lucky to have you. Please relax, you are safe here, you are loved here, and most importantly, you are healed here.

The fire crackles and begins to flourish. The druid puts a grate over the fire and adds a teapot, the flames only rarely lick the bottom. A Scottish thistle tea will cure what ails you. The teapot slowly begins to warm and eventually boil, whilst you take in the breathtaking views of Glen Coe.

The druid explains the strength of the Scottish people as they prepare the tea, with honey. The things they have survived, the weather they have endured, and even had a wall built by the Romans to keep the Scots in! They have the resilience, knowledge and community to outlast anything. If they can do it, so can you.

The tea is now prepared and the mug is being passed to you. Slàinte mhath [pronounced slanj ma va] and down the hatch it goes, as you drink deeply. A lovely, sweet tea warms you from the inside out. The druid waves his hand over you back and forth, speaking in gaelic [scottish gaelic – GAH-LIC] offering healing and blessings to your health. The druid asks you to inhale deeply, in through your nose and exhaling through your mouth. You are repeating this twice. inhale deeply, in through your nose and exhaling through your mouth. Inhale deeply, in through your nose and exhaling through your mouth. Now, the druid will create an energy field for you to tap into, and help you manifest using words of affirmation. Think of it as thoughts getting a signal boost.

Repeat these affirmations **either internally or aloud**:

“I am healthy.”

“I find it easy to make healthy choices for myself.”

“Each night when I sleep, my healing light accelerates my cellular regeneration.”

“This tea and blessing will encourage and support my good health infinitely.”

“I actively repel illness.”

“My high vibration keeps my mind, body and spirit protected and healthy.”

“I eat well and sleep well.”

“I attract people with my best interests at heart.”

“My mental health is paramount.”

“I trust myself and care for myself.”

“I enjoy taking care of my body.”

“My body deserves the best.”

You attract health and abundance, You seek and create healthy environments. You operate on the frequencies of healing and abundance. Each night when you sleep, you heal yourself deeply. You can tap into this power wherever and whenever.

The tea and ceremony is over, you feel so well it is euphoric. You are refreshed and rejuvenated by this experience. You slowly wander back through the forest, leaves crunching as you meander along the path. In the distance you spot a stag, and you both hold eye contact for a moment. He bows his head, as do you, and he slowly walks off. You are so blessed and supported.

You finally reach the door, but before you leave you take a deep breath in and on the exhale, thank the druid and the glen for a wonderful life experience.

Having come out the last door, a small gust of wind hits you and brings your awareness back to your body. Breathing deeply in and out, think about what you have learned today. Bring awareness to gratitude and new ideas,

Before leaving you catch your reflection in a mirror at the base of the stairs and are surprised how well you look. You are positively glowing. Your eyes are sparkling, your cheeks have a rosy glow. You look alive and well, thriving! What a journey you have been on, experiencing a new world beyond each door. Take this new found knowledge with you and apply it. You are a master manifestor!

You take this opportunity to breathe deeply in through your nose and out through your mouth, rebalancing yourself before climbing the steps back up into the manor.

One, you are becoming aware of your power

Two, you are shaking off the old ways of thinking

Three, there has been a shift in your mindset

Four, every aspect of your life is in balance

Five, major changes are on the way

Six, you are so much health and wealth to share

Seven, your luck is made and is an infinite resource

Eight, you are becoming more aware of your body

Nine, you are more aware of your breath

Ten, you are back in the hallway and feel your feet on the marble floor.You slowly pace back, past the many rooms, sculptures and lush, green plants. You hear your footsteps echo as you wander along the beautiful marble hallway.

Feeling refreshed and ready to manifest your best life, you take in this incredible hallway once more. You now know what you want to physically manifest, whether it is a home like this or a secluded cabin in the woods. Only you can make it happen. You head out of the manor, so grateful for the lessons you have learned today, and climb into the back seat of the car, exhausted but satisfied. The car moves off, gravel crackling underneath the tyres, and the flowers from the garden sway in the wind, almost as though they are waving “goodbye for now.”

You are enough. You are grateful. You are loved.

As we come to the end of this guided meditation, I ask you to bring awareness to your breath, and allow it to fill up your body with active energy. You feel so refreshed and rejuvenated, full of yourself in the best way. Be kind and gentle with yourself for the hour following this guided meditation. Please consume a glass of water, and a small snack if you are hungry. Thank you for being here today and taking this time for yourself. It is an act of bravery in this world.

Guided Meditation Four

Welcome to your guided meditation, my name is ______. Please allow yourself to get comfortable, whether that's sitting down or lying down with a blanket. Please do not drive or operate machinery whilst listening to this guided meditation. Close your eyes and let's begin.

You awaken in a room full of pink clouds, it is a sunset in a bedroom and you immediately feel safe and secure.

You are here to express gratitude.

There is a mirror with a lovely mat in front of it, adorned with blankets. Are you ready to talk to yourself?

The vibration of gratitude aids your abundance and your ability to manifest. By being grateful you're showing the universe but you are thankful for what you have and what you are about to receive.

Take a deep breath into your nose and out through your mouth, we will begin with a full body scan.

Take this opportunity to settle into your body and bring awareness to any areas that feel stressed.

Where in your body are you feeling stressed? take another deep breath through your nose and on the exhale imagine all the stress leaving your body, let all your burdens float away as you exhale through your mouth.

Wherever you're sitting or lying down, let the furniture or the ground meet you and allow your body to sink. Where all the tension from your muscles relax and allow the energy inside you to calm
down. Let the energy ebb and flow like the calm sea. You feel more relaxed with each wave that passes through you.

As you inhale, roll your neck down to your right hand side where the chin meets the shoulder. Feel your neck stretch out and let out a deep satisfying breath. Slowly bring your neck back to your mid position and have your chin touch your chest. Take another breath in through your nose and then roll your neck so that your head is pointing towards your left shoulder and again your chin will meet your shoulder. Feel the going through your neck and exhale through your mouth. Your shoulders are stretched and now they drop tension free and relaxed.

Looking in the mirror, you can see the difference in your shoulders and facial expression as you begin to relax more and more.

We next bring awareness to the tight jaw, take a deep breath in by yawning and allow your mouth to stretch open and on the exhale yawn loudly breathing outwards and moving the jaw back to closed
position.

Stick your tongue at your mouth through closed lips, like you used to do as a child. Feel the small stretch in your jaw then relax and exhale through your mouth. Taking another deep breath in, you stretch out each hand in front of you and wiggle your fingers. You move your wrists in circular motions and you even hear some cracking and popping which is normal. Allow the tingles to come as you move your hands from a fist position to an open palm position, moving the hand back and forth, both stretching and relaxing. Finally, give them a shake and exhale through your mouth. Raise your hands above your head and stretch out taking in a deep breath at the same time. Feel your back stretch out and feel all the tension release, try to do this in the morning when you first wake up.

Now bring awareness to your hips and pelvis, do they feel tight at all? Breathe deeply and move your legs into a basket, pigeon pose or any type of pose that stretches out the hip. We are going to take 3 deep breaths.

On the 1st breath breathe in through your nose and stretch out your left hip.

Feel the stretch and let all the stress out on the exhale. On the second breath bring awareness to your centre, does your left head feel better? take a deep breath in through the nose and exhale through the mouth. On the third breath stretch out the right hip, on the exhale moving back to centre.

Your hips are feeling looser and far more comfortable. You put your legs straight in front of you and reach to touch your toes. On the inhale, reach for your toes and hold them for 3 2 1 and release your breath as you return upright. We will repeat this pose again. as you inhale, reach down towards your toes and feel the deep stretch through your calves and your hamstrings. Exhale and return to the sitting up position.

Finally bring awareness to your feet by wiggling your toes then moving your ankles in a clockwise position. Take a deep breath in through your nose and exhale through your mouth.

You're so calm and relaxed. You're thinking about all the times you have felt joy and about the people you spent those times with. you remember these times fondly and they're so grateful that they happened. Take a moment to think about and experience where you couldn't stop laughing or had the biggest smile on your face.

Look in the mirror and see your smile. What an amazing smile!

Think about the company you were with, can you think of something nice about each person who was there? Whether this is a physical compliment or you admire them for their emotional vulnerability or academic achievements. If there are too many people, think of three.

If the roles were reversed what are three things you would be complimented on? Take a moment to think about this and breathe through any uncomfortable sensations that may arise. Do you find it hard to receive compliments but find it easy to give them? Let the universe crack open your heart chakra. You deserve to be appreciated and acknowledged.

Your entire existence is valid.

[pause]

Regardless of your gender or sexuality, you are loved. Regardless of your status or wealth, you are loved.

No matter the colour of your skin or religion, you are loved. You are not afraid to express gratitude. you're thankful for every single day. Whether you're thanking someone for an act of service at your local coffee shop, Or feel relieved a burden being lifted, you are grateful. You are so in love with yourself. you are so full of love for yourself. you consistently pour into your own cup, Which then allows you to pour into other people. The longest relationship you will ever have is with yourself.

You look at your body in the mirror, appreciating it and taking it all in. How divine you are!

You love every inch of your body. you are so grateful for the places you have been in this body. Your body is composed of muscle, fat and water. Every single person has the same building blocks; they are just stacked differently. Everybody has a great body. You love your body on days when it is hard and on days when it's easy. You love your body when it's exhausted and when it's at its peak performance.

On a daily basis your body does incredible things. Each night when you go to bed, your body repairs itself and commits learning to long term memory. The brain is actually very active at night. As you dream your body is repaired at a cellular level. Your mind is repaired during deep sleep, where it is silent And also in REM sleep which helps emotional processing.

You're so grateful for the deep healing you experience on a nightly basis where you're taken to the higher realms by angels taking care of you using light waves. Your entire light body is being purged of any negative energies and this higher realm.

You can call upon this at any time and invoke the healing powers. You can heal yourself and also heal others by thinking positively and seeking help when you require it. It is incredibly brave to ask for help or reach out when you are struggling the most. Your mental health is paramount and it is important that you maintain your health. Take this opportunity to breathe and appreciate all that you have overcome to get to this point.

Think about the things that you have struggled with that you no longer perceive as a struggle, what has changed for you?

Have you stopped to thank yourself for getting yourself out of an unhappy situation? This is the time to thank yourself.

You have weathered every storm and have achieved new heights at every turn. You have managed stormy seas and stayed afloat when you thought you were drowning.

Show yourself gratitude in the form of a deep breath and inhaling through your nose, stretching out your abdomen and holding the breath in your body. On the exhale, breathe out gratitude. How can you show yourself more compassion in your day to day life? Hey, can you show the kindness that you show strangers to yourself? Would you speak to your best friend the way you speak to yourself internally? If not, take a moment to think about why.

Can you identify the voice that criticises you? Often it is the voice of a caregiver, or authority figure who was not emotionally available or was very harsh. Realise that this person is not you, so why are you allowing them to criticise you so fiercely inside your own head? You are retraining your brain and taking back control. Every time you hear this critical voice, that is not yours, ask them why they have the audacity to speak up? Why do they get an opinion when they are from the past and don't know you any more? They really do live in the mind rent free and you have the power to evict them.

How do you like to be addressed? Do you like your name? If not, what would you change it to? If so, take a moment to feel gratitude you are in alignment with your given name.

How do you like to be spoken to? How do you speak to people? Can you think of a time where someone really stopped to listen and communicate with you? How did that make you feel? Breathe through any uncomfortable emotions that arise.

You're now challenging every thought that comes to mind, and asking if it serves you in any way. The first thought is our social programming and conditioning and the second one that follows is our true self. You have the opportunity to break your social programming with each thought. Ask each thought that arises how it serves you and listen for a response.

Who do you want to be? How are you going to get there whilst loving yourself? Practise gratitude for where you are now and where you're heading to, life happens all the time and there is no perfect time to "'begin" something, so go for it!

It is important to let people go when the relationship no longer serves us. It doesn't matter if this is a family relationship, a friendship or a romantic partnership, if it makes you unhappy then let them go. Equally sometimes you might make someone unhappy and this is a great opportunity to reset your boundaries and work on any toxic traits, because every human being has them. There is always an opportunity for personal growth in the positive and negative aspects of life, to maintain detachment, view them as lessons and watch your mindset change.

The only thing that never changes is the fact that everything changes.

Detachment means that although you care, and are committed, you understand that certain things are best left up to the universe, and what is for you will not go by you.

You are not possessive of people or things.
Practise detachment and gratitude and manifestation will come easily to you. Be thankful like it is already yours or the event has already

happened. You only attract, you do not chase. Everything that is for you is on the way to you.

Affirmations to express gratitude for your physical health, this can be spoken **either internally or aloud**:

“I am so grateful for the wonderful things I have and can achieve in this body.”

“I feel so healthy and well.”

“My body and I are in alignment.”

“I love to nourish and care for my body.”

Affirmations to express gratitude for your emotional availability and vulnerability:

“I am not afraid to be vulnerable.”

“I know emotions are human and in feeling those emotions, I have nothing to be ashamed for.”

“I can express myself freely.”

“I open myself up so that others may open up too.”

Repeat these affirmations spoken **either internally or aloud to** express gratitude for your psychic gifts and spiritual healing:

“I am so grateful for my third eye opening.”

“My spiritual awakening has brought me so many blessings.”

“My intuition is on point.”

You look in the mirror and see your aura. What colours can you see? If people only ever saw your light body, how differently would you be described? It is time to make the inner and outer match. Be your authentic self. Dress how you want to dress. Love yourself and others who bring joy to your life and want you to grow.

If you could talk to yourself as a child, imagine they were sitting right in-front of you at a pivotal age, the age where something changed. What loving words would you tell them? What would you have wanted to be told? Use this space to comfort your inner child, hold them, cry with them, whatever you both need.

Keep breathing deeply as emotions and memories bubble to the surface. You do not have to engage with any memory that brings discomfort. Acknowledge its presence, thank yourself for raising awareness and let it go for emotional release.

There is no shame in crying. There is no shame in sobbing or wailing. Releasing the emotions now serves you far better in the long run. You do not need to be strong. You just need to feel what you are feeling and express the emotions. Sometimes, we need to feel emotions that have been pushed down very deep, because in truth, they are a thorn in our side. You do not need to carry this burden, and shame is the gatekeeper that prevents you from dropping it off and leaving it in the past.

Notice where these emotions are resonating in the body? Many people feel deep sadness in their chest. Can you identify what is happening right now for you? As we work through this together, please know that you are doing a wonderful job. You are putting in the hard work, loving yourself and making the effort to be well and healthy. Your inner child is delighted, they feel so connected to you. All the parts of yourself are so proud of you. They are applauding you and cheering you on through this difficult moment, and remind you that moments are just that, fleeting.

To feel joy and happiness, one must know sadness and despair. But you do not need to sit with the latter for long. With your new mindset, you understand that expressing emotions at the time is not a weakness, but an incredible strength. The courage it takes to shed a tear when the people around you are afraid to cry or show any vulnerability. It is brave to smile at strangers and show your joy outwardly, people might find it odd at first, until you inspire them to do the same thing.

Feeling the goosebumps on your skin from music, hearing a song that moves you to tears is a small fragment of the human experience. What else makes you shiver? What resonates with you?

Perhaps it is a video on social media, where an animal is saved and becomes a house-hold favourite, one of the family. Or you see someone trying and failing at a new trick on their skateboard, and admire their ambition and tenacity which reminds you to never give up. No matter how big or small, notice what resonates with you. Notice the things that feed your soul. Is it singing loudly on the drive home with the volume all the way up? Not caring who sees or hears you? Because that is a joy and a moment of self care.

Baking a cake for a loved one and eating some batter off the spoon is not selfish. You are pure creation and are making something from scratch. Enjoy the sweetness and the fruits of your labour, because that is your reward. A moment alone in the kitchen, the cake smells wonderful as it bakes in the oven and you enjoy a hot drink and lick the spoon. You shiver in delight, because it tastes good!

Whatever it may be, add these ingredients to your life. Your inner child has plenty of ideas if you are willing to listen. Let us take the time to listen now, so we may implement changes and improve your life, immediately.

Take in a deep breath through your nose, and exhale through your mouth. Listen. You may be a visual person and the inspiration comes to you as an image, no matter how your brain works, the message will come through. You can access your inner child at any time. What are they saying right now?

This was a wonderful healing experience, and a lesson in gratitude. You realise you have so much in the way of blessings and have so much to offer your community and the world. Your spirit shines so brightly and is a beacon of hope and inspiration for others. Will you tell yourself that? Can you imagine what the next generation of children will be like, if they speak to themselves kindly with words of affirmation?
The pink clouds begin to move round the room carrying wonderful words that describe you. You close your eyes and commit this day to memory, for it is always with you when you are struggling.

You are enough. You are grateful. You are loved.

As we come to the end of this guided meditation, I ask you to bring awareness to your breath, and allow it to fill up your body with active energy. You feel so refreshed and rejuvenated, full of yourself in the best way. Be kind and gentle with yourself for the hour following this guided meditation. Please consume a glass of water, and a small snack if you are hungry. Thank you for being here today and taking this time for yourself. It is an act of bravery in this world.

Guided Meditation Five

Hello and welcome to this guided meditation. We will be focusing on removing energy blockages that interfere with soulmate connections; the side effects of this guided meditation include a purging of intense emotions. This meditation is designed to bring your emotions and triggers to the surface to be felt and integrated.

This healing then puts you in a higher vibrational state attracting a soul mate who is on your level. You may already be with a soul mate, and if this is the case, this guided meditation will help clear stagnant energies within the relationship and allow the love to flow freely again.

You are a beautiful soul, and you are pure love and light. There may have been a time where you didn't feel as such; that moment may be now. Your guides, and I know that you are so deserving of the love that you give to people.

You are about to have your cup overflowing with love and abundance.

First, let us begin by creating a ball of white light in the ball of our hands-feeling the energy in the shape of a sphere. Release the ball from your hands. This orb floats up and hovers above your head, shining down from above.

Feel the gentle warmth radiate down, like the sun on a summer's morning. The orb moves through you in waves, and with each wave, you feel lighter and happier. You inhale deeply through your nose, allowing the breath to fill up your chest can't and lower abdomen. You slowly exhale out your mouth, pushing the air out, and the chest compresses in again.

Now that the light waves have cleared all basic energy blockages, we can focus on the stagnation around the heart chakra, sacral and root chakras.

Focusing on the white orb hovering above, move it down through the body all the way to the root chakra at the base of the spine. Think about a time when you felt confident or secure. Use this to lock in the feeling of security, which is the primary purpose of the root chakra.

We must stay grounded. You are safe and secure; you have everything you'll ever need inside of you waiting to be accessed. This blockage has been removed. You love all of you so deeply; you know that you are complete, and a partner is a lovely gift from the universe to go through life with. People will come and go, but you will remain unmoved but constantly evolving through your relationships.

The white healing orb floats upwards to the sacral chakra, which describes our creativity, sexuality and openness to intimacy. The orb pulses sending deep healing, particularly to those who have a womb- extra love is sent through the sacral chakra and resonates deeply through the uterus. Those with wombs have now released the blockages to their creativity. Your sexuality is valid. Your expression of your sexuality is innate to you. Although we must recognise others struggles and minorities, remember, the foundation of all relationships, whether they are hetero-normative or LGBTQIA+, is love!

Love is universal and is for everyone. If you are suppressing areas of your sexuality, you can express them here in this safe healing space. Let's take a moment to sit with any feelings that may arise here.

[2-minute pause]

It doesn't matter your sexual orientation, as long as you are open to giving and receiving love from a consenting partner. The orb has shone its light during your thinking time, healing and transforming the sacral chakra so that you can be intimate and vulnerable when you desire to be.

Once more, the orb rises past the solar plexus and stops, sinking into the heart chakra. Allow the light to crack the chakra open; so many of us have hardened our hearts to love - it’s time to re-open it. If you seek love, you must be able to handle the transformative nature of love. For some, receiving love is the most challenging obstacle to overcome because they have never felt the intensity of true unconditional love. Your guides know it's intense, but you can transmute anything. You can direct the energy flow, sending it around the body or offering yourself protection and healing. Love is an ingredient and a tool, use it your way to keep your heart open.

How do you like to be loved? How do you give love? Is your heart open to compromise? There are many questions to ask ourselves when it comes to matters of the heart. When you fall for someone, will you fall freely? Or teeter upon the edge, skirting around the edges of a more profound love?

The blockages around the heart chakra have been removed. We now have the free flow of energy through the chakras closely involved with love, and the heart chakra is open. It is now time to manifest. Repeat these affirmations either internally or verbally. These affirmations can be used daily to help align your love life with the highest good, allowing the universe to guide you to what is yours:

" I am deserving of an incredible partner; my partner is worthy of me because they too are incredible."

" I do not chase love; I attract."

" The partner I seek also seeks me."

"I love myself unconditionally."

Whenever you feel out of alignment, use these affirmations to get back on track. You are truly a magnetic being and those of a high vibration feel called to you. You will continue to heal and raise your vibration; you are love and light.Your chakras are free flowing and you can feel the difference. You did an amazing job today, well done you.

Thank you for listening to this guided meditation to remove energy blockages and welcome union with your soul mate, I am here when you need me. Namaste.

Reiki Guided Meditation

Hello, my name is _______ welcome back to another guided meditation.

Today's guided meditation is a reiki session, which can be accessed anytime. It is not recommended to drive or operate machinery whilst listening to guided meditations.

Here is a little background information before we begin our session today: Reiki originates from Japan, and has been used for centuries as a healing practice. Today I will be manipulating energy and drawing it out, like venom from a wound. I will use my technique to reset your energies and bring about healing, with your consent of course. This technique is powerful, please ensure that you have the time and space to relax afterwards as you will possibly feel sleepy or floaty. Please hydrate yourself and consume a small snack after this session as it is a big energetic shift.

Are you happy to go ahead with our session today?

Oh great! I am so glad we can continue with our session today. Let's get started.

We begin in a calm room, and sit on the cushions placed on the tatami mat. You can even lie damn if you so desire. The light floods in through the fusuma, a sage green paper door. In one corner of the room, there is a large bonsai tree and in another, a collection of crystals and burning incense.

Take a deep breath in and exhale through your mouth. You are welcome and safe here.
I am here to help you and use the Reiki techniques to re-centre your alignment and make you feel good! I am so proud of you for showing up for yourself. Creating time for deep healing is a necessity in this day and age. Sit or lie on the cushions and allow your body to sink into them. You are supported here physically and emotionally.

The technique I am using is like someone pulling a rope, an invisible rope that is centred in you for a moment. Using this rope I begin to pull on it, which then starts a powerful healing reaction. As the rope pulls, all the negativity that has been clouding your energy is being drawn out of you physically. Just because you can't see it, doesn't mean it's not happening.

Feel all the stagnation go as your energy begins to flow freely again. Your energy field has been cleansed, all energies that don't belong to you are sent back to their rightful owner. It's time to call back yours too, "all my energy returns to me". The rope falls away and the benefits of this technique will be felt for weeks.

Now, I move my fingers up and down the air, as if I'm tapping on glass, my fingers are locking in healing properties to your aura, to further assist the process before closing back down. Our hands raise together but do not touch, you can feel the energy palm to palm- "with this shared energy, I create a protective bubble that repels negativity. Returning it to whomever sent it, with love and light.

You slowly open your eyes and your awareness returns. You notice instantly that a great weight has been removed from your being. You feel as though your spirit has had the most amazing bubble bath, you feel so clean and refreshed. You notice the feel of the cushions under you and the firmness of the tatami mat under them. You slowly begin to stretch out once more and begin to stand up slowly. Bending over and touching your toes, slowly draw your fingertips up the shins and knees, feeling the stretch in the quad muscles and hamstrings. Now, reaching up slowly towards the sky, put your arms up from either side then allow them to stretch fully above your head. Feel the stretch in your spine and neck. You are now fully standing and we bow to each other as an act of mutual respect.

Our short Reiki healing session has come to an end, it was a pleasure to have you here. Please come back whenever you need a top up!

References

https://www.thehindubusinessline.com/blink/explore/the-tuning-of-electric-suns/article9790868.ecehttps://www.g-casa.com/conferences/shanghai/paper_pdf/Liu-mindcontrol.pd

fhttps://interestingengineering.com/the-radio-network-that-allowed-communication-with-submarines

https://www.ncbi.nlm.nih.gov/pmc/articles/PMC6037432/https://www.ncbi.nlm.nih.gov/pmc/articles/PMC5897318/https://www.ncbi.nlm.nih.gov/pmc/articles/PMC7642138/

https://www.iarc.who.int/wp-content/uploads/2018/07/pr208_E.pdf

https://pubmed.ncbi.nlm.nih.gov/31031095/

http://soundofgoldenlight.com/432-hz/

https://www.globalrecharge.guru/portfolio/432hz-om-chanting-3-hours/

https://meditativemind.org/528hz-miraculous-healing-frequency/

https://pubmed.ncbi.nlm.nih.gov/30414050/

https://www.frontiersin.org/articles/10.3389/fnhum.2018.00387/full

https://www.healthline.com/health/what-is-dmt#takeaway

https://drugpolicy.org/issues/brief-history-drug-war

https://medium.com/@ioannis.tsiokos/hoodoo-vs-voodoo-c9da8d5c193b

https://www.mathsisfun.com/numbers/nature-golden-ratio-fibonacci.html

https://medium.com/@allevity/they-killed-alan-watts-quote-8b5f388730fc

https://deepluciddreaming.com/2020/12/yoga-nidra-for-lucid-dreaming-wild/

https://www.alittlesparkofjoy.com/telepathy/

http://www.bbc.co.uk/earth/story/20141111-plants-have-a-hidden-internethttp://blog.virgovault.com/2012/10/02/fixed-star-algol-25-taurus-sexual-emotional-psychological-drives-heterosexual-men-algol/

https://www.constellationsofwords.com/algol/

https://www.skyscript.co.uk/algol.html

Open Astron. 2018; 27: 232–263 Research Article Sebastian Porceddu*, Lauri Jetsu, Tapio Markkanen, Joonas Lyytinen, Perttu Kajatkari, Jyri Lehtinen, and Jaana Toivari-Viitala Algol as Horus in the Cairo Calendar: the possible means and the motives of the observations https://doi.org/10.1515/astro-2018-0033 Received Feb 15, 2018; accepted May 04, 2018

https://astrologyking.com/fixed-star-sirius/

https://www.interlochenpublicradio.org/news/2019-08-26/sirius-and-the-flooding-of-the-nile-this-week-on-the-storytellers-night-sky

https://www.bbc.co.uk/bitesize/articles/zngsqp3

https://www.cacaomama.com/history-spirit/

https://ceremonial-cacao.com/pages/what-is-cacao-ceremony

https://www.ayahuascachurches.org/learn-all-about-ayahuasca-by-kahpi/

https://fabledchild.com/ramble/nelson/

https://malala.org/malalas-story

https://www.theguardian.com/world/commentisfree/2021/feb/04/nanaia-mahuta-new-zealands-maori-foreign-minister-is-the-perfect-diplomat

https://rainbowresourcecentre.org/files/16-08-Two-Spirit.pdf

https://shamandurek.com/

https://www.outofstress.com/what-does-deja-vu-mean-spiritually/

https://www.spiritanimal.info/deer-spirit-animal/

https://hibiscusmooncrystalacademy.com/lab-created-vs-natural-crystals/

https://www.delamora.life/cymatics

https://www.assignmentpoint.com/science/physics/amethyst.html

https://www.bohindiestream.com/blogs/bohindie-stream-writings/crystal-focus-selenite

https://healsomethinggood.com/chart-vibration-frequencies/

https://www.holisticshop.co.uk/articles/guide-pendulum-dowsing

https://www.generatorathletelab.com/blog/2019/12/5/chromotherapy-healing-or-hooey

https://tribaltradeco.com/blogs/teachings/what-is-a-spirit-animal#:~:text=Also%20known%20as%20a%20spirit,sacred%20place%20in%20tribal%20culture.

https://en.wikipedia.org/wiki/Barney_and_Betty_Hill

https://allthatsinteresting.com/alien-abductions/6

https://sabriyeayana.com/ascended-master-twin-flames/

https://www.youtube.com/watch?v=dDgr4uvet-g

https://www.thespruce.com/should-you-talk-to-your-plants-3972298

https://www.history.com/topics/british-history/stonehenge#:~:text=In%20the%2017th%20century%2C%20archaeologist,primitive%20graves%20at%20the%20site.

https://www.wionews.com/science-technology/roswell-crash-pentagon-admits-testing-wreckage-from-ufo-crashes-363656

https://www.smithsonianmag.com/smithsonian-institution/in-1947-high-altitude-balloon-crash-landed-roswell-aliens-never-left-180963917/

https://www.theguardian.com/science/2021/jun/23/scientists-identify-29-planets-where-aliens-could-observe-earth

https://news.sky.com/story/new-life-detection-tool-could-help-humans-find-alien-life-say-scientists-12315811

https://nymag.com/intelligencer/article/trump-ufo-moments.html

https://www.newscientist.com/definition/lsd/

https://medium.com/human-witch/consider-working-with-a-deity-d873fcb0f378

https://gleewood.org/seeking/doing/relationships-with-deities/

https://otherworldlyoracle.com/how-to-start-working-with-a-goddess-or-god/

https://www.sciencedirect.com/science/article/pii/B9781483166711500265

https://www3.dbu.edu/mitchell/biblical.htm

https://books.google.co.uk/books?id=m3EAAAAAMAAJ&pg=PA87&redir_esc=y#v=onepage&q&f=false

https://www.out.com/activism/2019/8/24/satanic-temple-says-it-will-fight-death-lbgtq-rights

https://the-demonic-paradise.fandom.com/wiki/King_Solomon

https://verdelljessup.com/the-3-types-of-entities-and-how-to-know-if-you-have-one/

https://drlesleyphillips.com/health-and-vitality/spiritual-entity/

https://www.washingtonpost.com/posteverything/wp/2016/07/01/as-a-psychiatrist-i-diagnose-mental-illness-and-sometimes-demonic-possession/

https://www.wikihow.com/Get-Rid-of-Demons

https://www.mtholyoke.edu/courses/rschwart/hist257/stephwhit/final/exorcism_pro.html

https://www.cabinetmagazine.org/issues/12/warner.php

https://wicca.wikia.org/wiki/Familiar

https://www.rituals.com/en-gb/mag-spirituality-full-moon.html

CPSIA information can be obtained
at www.ICGtesting.com
Printed in the USA
LVHW010324070422
715519LV00008B/150

9 781801 346740